# Longman Brain Trainer

**Practical and immediately useful advice on learning and revision for GCSE**

JONATHAN O'BRIEN

LONGMAN

Addison Wesley Longman Ltd,
Edinburgh Gate, Harlow,
CM20 2JE, England
and Associated Companies throughout the World



First published 1999

ISBN 0 582 36874 X

British Library Cataloguing-in-Publication Data

A catalogue record for this book is available from the British Library.

Set by 38

Printed in Great Britain by Henry Ling Ltd at The Dorset Press, Dorchester, Dorset.

# Contents

# Introduction

## Longman brain trainer

### The comprehensive and rapid guide to successful GCSE revision and exams

**'How can this text really help me?'**

**'Will it help me quickly and permanently improve my revision?'**

The purpose of this text is to help you be more **immediately** successful with your studying. This is not a typical text book for your GCSE subjects, it's a collection of ideas, advice, tips and techniques to help you take far greater control over your revision. It will save you time! It will make your revision more effective!

All you have to do is go through Part One which will take a few minutes (but could save you hours!). Here you will discover **how your brain learns best**!

*The skills explained in this text apply to **all** your subjects and you can choose which skills and techniques you want to use (normally those that you like most and work best for you!).*

We know that you have many subjects and plenty of coursework to concentrate on and there will be many other activities that make up your busy life. These ideas will help you achieve everything you want to do (and **have** to do) more successfully.

*Once learnt, these skills will be with you **for life** so it's a worthwhile investment in your future.*

This text is not just a quick way of solving your immediate GCSE revision problems – it will help you save time and gain greater success and you will benefit by feeling happier and more motivated.

*You can help yourself and help your teachers to help you. This text presents all the information together in a complete programme that is easy and quick to use.*

## ★ What is revision?

To many people revision is merely memorising information in the last few weeks before the exams – but there is much more to revision than that.

It's about:

- understanding and organising information and ideas so you can learn them easier
- recognising a topic question and knowing how to plan and answer it
  (both of these will help you memorise the facts better)
- using strategies and techniques for remembering
- using and gaining **experience**. If you start early enough and plan your time well you will begin to find that your memory is expanding, you will think faster and make links more easily

***Use this text and you will begin to recognise many benefits:***

- you will have a larger, faster memory
- you will improve your problem solving skills
- you will increase your own motivation as you realise these skills are improving your results
- you will feel in control of your life and revision
- you will feel less worried and more reassured about your learning
- you will learn how to organise everything you have to do and want to do
- you will gain heightened confidence and a 'feel good' factor!
- you will find your tasks become easier to do and also more interesting

## ★ How to use this text

This text can help you **now**.

**Read Part One** – it will take you a few minutes.

**Steadily work through Part Two** – just a few minutes spent familiarising yourself with the skills will give you the overall picture, then you can focus on the areas that concern you most when you need them.

You should also think how these ideas will apply to your own subjects. There are examples of how these have been used by others in a variety of subjects – the individual *Longman Study Guides* will also tell you more.

Stop and think occasionally just how you might be able to use one skill or another. For instance, when you need to concentrate on revision notes or exam answers, you can turn to these sections and dip in and out of them. It won't take long and will immediately help you focus your mind.

**Use Part Three** to concentrate on developing your exam skills.

Read through it, highlight your main areas of weakness and plan what you need to do to improve in these areas.

Discuss your strengths and weaknesses with your teachers, tutor, parents or friends; use their knowledge of you to help you identify the areas you need to work on.

Begin to organise **how** you can help yourself.

> *Remember: a small investment in time now, while you consider which style and techniques to use, will save you hours in the future. It could double the amount you achieve in your revision sessions!*

## ★ Test your situation now!

| Put a tick in the column that applies to you: | Strengths and weaknesses | | | |
|---|---|---|---|---|
| *Remember to answer honestly, as you've nothing to gain by cheating!* | **Yes** | **Mostly** | **Sometimes** | **Never** |
| 1. Do you know how to make yourself work, even when you really don't want to? | | | | |
| 2. Do you organise your day, work and free time so everything is done on time? | | | | |
| 3. Do you listen carefully in class and concentrate on every word? | | | | |
| 4. Do you always have a tidy, organised workplace? | | | | |
| 5. Do you make a plan for your work before you start? | | | | |
| 6. Do you make efficient, easy to remember notes, using key ideas or facts only? | | | | |
| 7. Do you find it easy to understand what 'The Question' is asking? | | | | |
| 8. Do you learn things off by heart easily and remember them when under pressure? | | | | |
| 9. Do you always check your work through when you've finished? | | | | |
| 10. Do you ask yourself why you're studying a topic – how it will be relevant later in life? | | | | |
| 11. Do you know how to read large chunks of text without going in to detail, so you don't find that the last bit was all you needed? | | | | |
| 12. Do you know how to stop yourself writing everything down word for word when taking notes, revising, preparing or writing an answer, in case it might be useful? | | | | |
| 13. Are you relaxed about revision and exams? | | | | |
| 14. Do you organise your notes and files so you know where everything is? | | | | |
| 15. Do you make a revision timetable at least eight weeks before exams? | | | | |
| 16. Do you stick to it? | | | | |
| 17. Do you know how to handle stress? | | | | |
| 18. Do you begin to revise early enough? | | | | |
| 19. Do you know how and why to avoid staying up late the night before the exam? | | | | |
| 20. Have you worked through past papers? | | | | |
| 21. Do you know where, when and how long each exam is? | | | | |
| 22. Do you build in a memory review cycle (see pages 24–25)? | | | | |
| 23. Do you look through the syllabus and cover each topic? | | | | |
| 24. Do you revise the topics you know least well first? | | | | |
| 25. Do you know how to work under pressure in an exam? | | | | |
| 26. Do you see learning and school as a 'stepping-stone' leading to a great future? | | | | |
| 27. Do you believe in yourself, think positively and remain confident? | | | | |
| 28. Do you want to be successful, in control of your life? | | | | |
| *Now add up the total number of ticks in each column* | | | | |
| **Total:** | | | | |

**Yes: More than 26** *a*) Brilliant, you don't need this book! or b) You're a liar!

**Mostly: More than 20** Good but read on, you'll learn something new.

**Sometimes: More than 15** Sounds as if you'd find some tips and techniques helpful. This book, your dedication and your teachers will help you improve!

**Never: More than 15** All is not lost if you start to change now. This book is definitely for you!

# Part 1
# Brain Power!

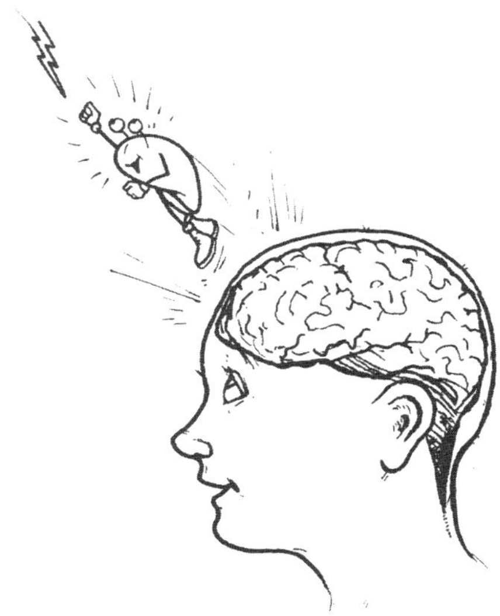



*This section will help you discover your own unique learning approach and personality. It will take you a few minutes to discover how to begin to use your brain better but the improvements are generally rapid and very stimulating and motivating. So Part One is well worth the investment in the time it takes to read through. And you will find that the rest of the text is that much more useful too!*

# Maximise your brain power

## Your unique brain

Your brain is divided into three parts. These have to be working in harmony to maximise your brain power.

- The **primitive brain** controls basic life functions – breathing, heartbeat, sleep, and body clock. Being stressed, tired and not eating properly can seriously affect your brain as its energy is directed towards maintaining the basic functions. This will undermine your ability to learn. You can help by identifying when you learn best, by being fit and by being relaxed.
- The **middle brain** controls emotions, moods, feelings and long-term memory. So having a positive attitude, feeling happy, confident and having a purpose will greatly improve your ability to learn and remember.
- The **thinking brain** is your intelligent brain – the grey matter. It is divided into two hemispheres – the left is your 'academic' brain and the right is your 'creative' brain.

**The two hemispheres receive and process *different* information**

| **Left hemisphere** *(mostly academic)* | **Right hemisphere** *(mostly creative)* |
|---|---|
| speech and words | spatial relationships |
| numbers | patterns |
| symbols | art and music |
| facts and detail | visual images |
| handwriting | meaning |
| 'conscious learning' | 'subconscious learning' |

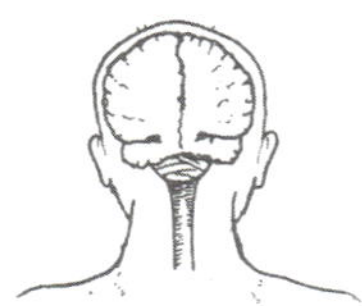

*Amazingly most people only use about 4% of their brain's capacity in their lifetime.*

Your brain is more powerful than any computer. It contains billions of cells capable of processing the information coming in from your senses – it's rather like a massive network of roads. The more connections you make in your brain by doing or learning things in as many ways as possible, the more routes your network will have and studying will become easier.

*It is easy to learn how to use your brain to make more connections which will help you to learn faster and make revision easier.*

You need to use your academic and your creative brains at the same time. This is called **whole brain learning**. You can do this by:

- knowing the advantages and disadvantages of your learning approach
- using your different intelligences by revising in different ways
- taking in information through your strongest learning channel
- repeating your learning in a variety of ways and getting your brain waves working

*Memory, thinking speed and understanding are greatly improved if the creative and academic brains are linked.*

**Learning should involve both hemispheres**. It is not enough to learn facts in an ordered, 'by rote' manner. If you involve your right side (colour, pattern, music, rhyme, creativity, intuition) you can learn and remember at least twice as effectively. To revise successfully each area has to be able to work properly and to balance with the other area. Understand your own brain and the way it likes to work and you unlock your own genius.

### *But why is it useful to you?*

- If we are more dominant in one hemisphere, it will affect the way we learn, our revision, our memory and our speed of thinking in an exam.
- If you don't use both halves at the same time you will revise twice as slowly.

So you need to know about your brain to help **your** exam performance.

## ★ Brain cells and memory connections

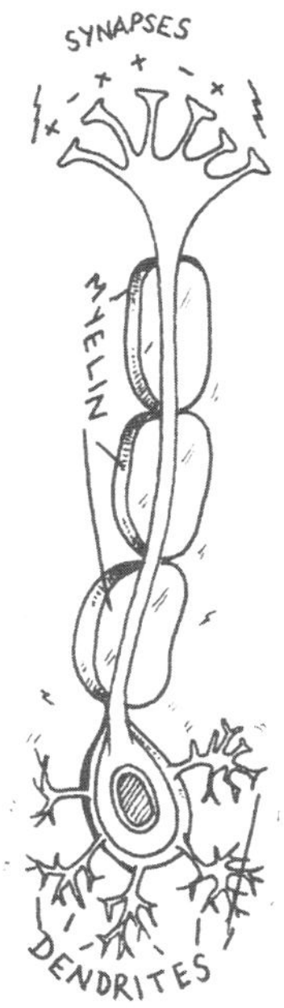


There are at least a billion individual neurons or nerve cells (otherwise known as the 'grey matter') in the brain. These are the pathways along which thoughts and sensations, in the form of electrical impulses or **brain waves**, are transmitted to their designated destination in the brain. These impulses contain information about your emotions and about everything you think, see, hear, taste, smell and touch.

Imagine your brain as a massive road map with your neurons ending in junctions known as dendrites. As more of these dendrites connect, the denser the network and the stronger your memory and 'knowledge' become.

***You can exercise your brain like a muscle – its capacity expands!***

When you learn something for the first time, a series of connections are made between your brain's neurons – a new pathway is formed. The more times you repeat a thought, or an action, the thicker the pathway becomes. The junctions are given an extra coat of a substance called **myelin** which protects the nerve but also acts as an insulator and increases the efficiency of the nerve's electrical impulse.

### Brain waves - conscious and subconscious learning

Brain waves work on four frequencies. They are the electric impulses that travel along brain cells, passing messages to each other.

| | |
|---|---|
| **Beta waves** | You are wide-awake. **Conscious learning** is happening. These are alert/active waves. |
| **Alpha waves** | These are **subconscious learning waves**. You are relaxed but alert. |
| **Theta waves** | These waves happen when you are in deep meditation or dreaming. They are very creative. They happen just before you go into a deep sleep or just before waking. |
| **Delta waves** | These are deep sleep waves. |

***How can this help you now?***

When you are reading, writing or concentrating you are using **Beta waves** and processing information in your **academic (left) hemisphere**.

Subconscious learning happens mainly through your **creative (right) hemisphere** when you are relaxed and your **Alpha brain waves** are buzzing.

You need to learn to work when both kinds of waves are active. This is the most efficient way to learn.

***Have you ever wondered why you can remember the words of a song or TV advertisement when you did not actually sit down and learn them?***

You do this by **subconscious learning**. Ways of exploiting this are:

- putting posters about what you are trying to learn around your room – so that they look like adverts
- speaking information while listening to music without words
- illustrating or highlighting your notes while reading up on a topic

Develop a routine and an environment that encourages the waves to flow!

> *Link the Web – connect your brain cells.*
> *Use it or lose it!*

## ★ Your learning personality

You may be a **skydiver learner** who prefers to get an overview of a topic, so that you can see the whole picture and where you're going before you start.

Or

You may be an **explorer learner** who prefers to work step by step as you go along, making decisions about where to go next at each stage.

**Which do you think you are? Tick or highlight the items in each list that seem to describe you**

*A **skydiver** begins with the whole in order to understand the parts.*

| **The high skydiver –** | ***but –*** |
|---|---|
| ❐ sees new ways of doing things | ❐ can forget important details |
| ❐ finds creative solutions | ❐ can be disorganised |
| ❐ sees long-term possibilities | ❐ delays before starting |
| ❐ sees the total picture – in 3D | ❐ doesn't criticise ideas well |
| ❐ is unhurried; doesn't worry too much | ❐ doesn't stick to plans |
| ❐ sees links between subjects/topics | ❐ only works in bursts |
| ❐ thinks of many new alternatives | ❐ forgets resources (e.g. books) |
| ❐ enjoys free-flowing writing | ❐ is easily distracted |
| ❐ has a feel for a subject | ❐ doesn't file or rework notes |
| ❐ enthuses others and is supportive | ❐ doesn't often plan in advance |
| ❐ uses lots of resources at once | ❐ rushes into answers without thinking |
| ❐ likes variety and excitement | ❐ tries to do too much at once |
| ❐ likes new experiences | ❐ doesn't work out priorities |
| ❐ skims through work very effectively | ❐ leaves things until the last minute |
| ❐ becomes totally involved in interesting topics | ❐ doesn't check work |
| ❐ tries new ideas and techniques | |
| ❐ uses trial and error | |

*An **explorer** starts with the parts in order to comprehend the whole.*

| **The intrepid explorer –** | **but –** |
|---|---|
| ❐ organises facts and materials well | ❐ needs too much information before starting work |
| ❐ sees links between ideas | ❐ doesn't consult teachers or friends enough |
| ❐ enjoys problems and their solutions | ❐ won't try new approaches |
| ❐ works things out well on paper | ❐ becomes too involved in theory |
| ❐ works well on own | ❐ can be set in his/her ways |
| ❐ is precise, thorough and meticulous | ❐ can be impatient |
| ❐ plans everyday work and revision well | ❐ sees only one way of doing something |
| ❐ sets clear goals and priorities | ❐ is often preoccupied with details |
| ❐ reworks notes and essay plans | ❐ is not especially creative/imaginative |
| ❐ isn't easily distracted | ❐ is poor at inventing questions |
| ❐ reads instructions carefully | ❐ doesn't work well with others |
| ❐ researches exam syllabus thoroughly | ❐ task completion important – not quality |
| ❐ likes to understand every aspect of a topic | |
| ❐ works step by step | |
| ❐ is good at finding and using resources | |

One approach is not necessarily better than another it's just that your approach will influence which revision techniques suit your understanding and your memory. You may well be a mixture of both types – using both approaches. However, you will probably start with your strongest tendency.

***Why is this important to you now?***

If you know which learning approach best suits you, you can plan your revision sessions around it.

It is very important for **all** learners to:

- have a simple overview of a topic **before** starting serious studying
- plan a step by step approach to their revision sessions and exam answers

Your own personality will dictate whether the Skydiver or Explorer in you dominates. You will learn how to avoid the more negative characteristics. **Good learning has to be a combination of both.**

## ★ You are very intelligent!

### Intelligence quotient (IQ)

The current belief is that you have at least eight intelligences and that they are linked to one hemisphere of the brain or the other: the more you use your whole brain the more your **intelligence quotient** (IQ) increases. This is called the **theory of multiple intelligence**.

| Intelligence | Good at ... |
|---|---|
| Linguistic | talking, writing, reading and linguistic skills |
| Mathematical/logical | numbers, systems, problem solving |
| Visual/spatial | how things look, imagination, presenting work |
| Practical | doing, building, touching, sport, hobbies, using hands |
| Musical | melody, rhythm, playing music, singing, creating tunes |
| Interpersonal | communicating well with others, developing a rapport |
| Intrapersonal | talking positively to yourself, self-analysis, being objective |
| Intuitive | perceiving information not obviously available – a sort of 'gut feeling' |

### Emotional quotient (EQ)

EQ concerns **emotional intelligence**. It's to do with behaviour, how hard you are prepared to work, how easy you are to work with, and the interpersonal and intrapersonal intelligences discussed above.

***Develop your intrapersonal skills***

Try to be emotionally self-aware. Try to manage your emotions so that they don't control you. Try to achieve a balance. For instance, try to replace negative attitudes with positive ones and focus on self-motivation and self-discipline.

***Develop your interpersonal skills***

*Remember that interruptions in our emotional lives can have a marked effect on our learning.*

At work and school, the ability to understand the feelings of others is an important part of establishing a rapport with them. Try to develop your people skills. Learn to handle relationships with those around you carefully and sensitively.

These intelligences are also talents. All intelligences are important. In the academic world, linguistic and mathematical intelligences are often the most valued but this is not always the case in the world at large.

*Using all your intelligences will increase your capacity for learning and help you find inventive solutions. This is a valuable life skill.*

# Multisensory revision

All information reaches our brain through our senses, when we are looking, feeling, doing, hearing, tasting and smelling; these are our **learning channels**.

When it comes to learning for exams we can split these channels into three distinct groups – **practical**, **visual** and **auditory**. Your revision will be improved if you use all your senses when you revise. This is especially successful when you lead with your dominant channel.

## ★ Which is your dominant sensory learning channel?

Please rate from 1–3 in order of importance to you. (If you can't decide between one and another, give them equal rating.) The highest rating is 1, the lowest is 3. If you add up your totals at the end, the column with the lowest score indicates your dominant channel.

*We learn best when we are relaxed and concentrating – that's when both Alpha and Beta waves are buzzing.*

*We also learn best when we link both hemispheres of the brain by learning in a **multisensory** or **global** way using all our senses.*

| I like to ... | Practical (hands on) | Visual | Auditory |
|---|---|---|---|
| **Learn** | ❒ Through practical activity | ❒ With pictures, diagrams, video, copying something | ❒ By listening – lectures, tapes, discussions |
| **Spell** | ❒ By writing it out to construct it | ❒ By seeing the spelling in my mind | ❒ By sounding it out (phonetically) |
| **Write** | ❒ Action-based, in paragraphs | ❒ Very descriptive passages | ❒ In direct speech, rhyme, rhythm |
| **Memorise information** | ❒ Repetitive doing (or undoing) | ❒ By imagining in pictures, pattern and colours. Writing out. | ❒ By repeating out loud. Listening. Oral tests. |
| **Relax** | ❒ By actively 'letting off steam' | ❒ By watching not doing, e.g. film, sports match | ❒ By listening, e.g. music, radio |
| **Communicate** | ❒ By gestures, body language which can reflect my mood/ feelings | ❒ By watching facial reactions; use metaphors and analogies | ❒ By detecting mood and information through tone of voice and plenty of listening |
| **Read** | ❒ Practical/action-based material – but not often | ❒ Material that has plenty of description | ❒ Speeches, plays, conversation, chatty material |
| **Try to recall information** | ❒ By focusing on action and feelings | ❒ Through images, scenes, faces, colour, pattern | ❒ Hearing, sounds, words, stories, examples |
| **Draw** | ❒ Action scenes | ❒ Descriptive scenes | ❒ Busy, 'noisy' scenes |
| **Hear** | ❒ Active material | ❒ Descriptive material | ❒ Rhythmic, rhymed music, poetry |
| **Total score** | ______ | ______ | ______ |

## ★ Typical characteristics of the dominant learning channels

### Visual people

Neat – tidy workplace
Like tidy work
Plan ahead
Like detail
Like to look good
Remember by visual imagery
Like metaphors/similes
Like pictorial lessons
Don't listen well
Day-dream often
Like an overall view
Draw, scribble, doodle
Prefer visual images to words
Say, 'That looks right to me'; 'I can see what you mean'; 'I can picture the scene'.

### Practical people

Like physical activity
Move a lot
Make and/or alter things
Remember by doing and undoing
Like action words
Use gestures
Fidget
Like close proximity
Need to visit a place to remember it
Speak quite slowly and often use such phrases as:
'Let's tackle the issue'; 'Run that by me'; 'I'll handle that'; 'I feel at home with this idea'.

### Auditory people

Talk to themselves, mouth words
Like speeches/singing aloud
Tell jokes
Prefer verbal instructions
Are easily distracted by noise
Listen well
Like lessons/lectures
Enjoy rhyme and rhythm
Remember by listening
Recall conversations
Chat, discuss, argue and speak well
Spell out loud
and often use such phrases as: 'That rings a bell'; 'Sounds great to me'.

***Which seems most like you? Tick or highlight those characteristics that apply to you.***

*No one is 'exclusively' in one mode alone. Some people will be evenly balanced between all three.*

## ★ Multisensory revision skills

### How can this help you now?

**If you're studying a topic, create your own combination from this list:**

**20 ways to revise using your sensory learning channels and intelligences**

1. **Rephrase** question/topic heading/problem. (Linguistic)
2. **Seek a logical path** through the topic. Break into 'bite size' chunks. Make a flow chart. (Mathematical)
3. **Highlight** main points/facts/headings. (Practical)
4. **Talk** your way through the task; 'What do I already know?' (Intrapersonal)
5. **Make a brainframe** (see page 37) or use index cards as you go (main point/fact only); use colours. (Visual)
6. **Visualise** in your mind's eye. Create a picture or a movie in your mind. (Visual)
7. **Use diagrams**, cartoons, charts or models. (Visual)
8. **Listen** to non-lyrical music. Create mnemonics (see pages 30, 35 and 40), rhymes, rhythm. (Musical)
9. **Speak** difficult parts out loud. (Auditory)
10. **Tape record** key ideas/facts. (Auditory)
11. **Plan** your time: 35–40 minutes maximum, then break. (Mathematical)
12. **Tick** each heading/subheading as you complete it/understand it. (Practical)
13. Keep some **movement** going. (Practical)
14. **Talk positively** to yourself – keep yourself going. (Intrapersonal)
15. **Build in rewards**. Praise yourself. (Intrapersonal)
16. **Discuss** with others, swap notes. (Interpersonal)
17. **Make a poster** of the key points of a topic. (Visual)
18. **Make a game** of the key facts. (Practical)
19. **Summarise** a topic. Make sure it is 'full enough' to make sense. (Linguistic)
20. Build in brief '**review time**' – what have I achieved? (Intrapersonal)

## ★ Multisensory intelligences in practice

Remember that there may be lots of different revision techniques above and beyond those already mentioned. Here are a few more examples related to subjects to help you begin to choose your own style.

| | |
|---|---|
| **Art** | Practise dealing with past topics; planning and producing finished work. |
| **Design and Technology** | Exam practice; use your visual memory to picture the processes you have been through. Use diagrams to remember the topics. |
| **Maths** | Define all the terms – prime number, square number and formulas. Make them into a game. Test a friend. Go through old papers. |
| **Religious Studies**<br>**History**<br>**Business Studies** | List the main facts, ideas and opinions. Create spidergrams to link ideas together. Make them in colour, hang them on your wall.<br>Make a summary of each topic, covering events, issues and evidence. |
| **English Literature** | Read the texts – highlight points in colour code for different characters. Make charts of evidence, quotes, themes, characters, plots, settings. |
| **English Language** | Make a list of your common spelling errors. List link words, practise different styles and different planning techniques. Practise comprehension and reading skills. |
| **Modern Languages** | Auditory learners will learn by the sound of the words – record them on tape. Repeat out loud. Visual learners may need to picture what the word looks like; look for words within words *mal-heureux* and root words with different endings *nous voyons/voyions*. Using a highlighter pen, pick out the patterns. Try to make associations with similar meanings in English, équipe – equipment – sport – team. |
| **Sciences** | Look for associations, e.g. *photosynthesis* – photo = light. *Homeostasis* – 'home and snug' implies all is well.<br>Invent stories, for instance to remember the parts and function of the kidney – 'My nephew (*nephron*), the regal (*renal*) and glamorous (*glomerulus*) Henry (*Henle*)'.<br>Pick out words and facts to learn and write them on to small cards. Play a game with a friend to guess their meaning. For example, words like: allele, meiosis, adenine, cytosine etc. (see *Longman Study Guide*).<br>Define general rules, e.g. Acid + alkali gives salt and water.<br>Make associations: 'a' is before 'e' as 1 is before 2 therefore alkane has 1 bond, alkene has 2 bonds. Alc*oh*ols contain OH. Recall experiments by visualising the apparatus used. Make charts of reactions with implications – if it's heavier is it more or less reactive?<br>Go through your *Longman Study Guide* and make a quiz using the summaries. Test a friend.<br>Make a summary chart of all the topics, including definitions, units, formulas and diagrams. Make 'key cards' or posters with key facts for visual learning. Practise drawing diagrams. |

*Choose whichever methods you feel work best for you.*

# Mind power

The state of your mind is vital to any success you may achieve. You only have to remember an occasion when something has gone really well to be able to see, hear and feel what it was like. We daydream of the future and remember the past – such dreams can bring a tear to the eye or a smile on our face. These dreams can put us in a positive or negative frame of mind. We can change our mood with our own thoughts and we can use this power to enhance our learning.

## ★ Self belief

If you believe you can succeed, you will; if you convince yourself you're going to fail, you can fail! Henry Ford is quoted as having said, 'Whether you think you can, or whether you think you can't, you're probably right.'

*Your mind is very powerful!*

Many of us in the past have thought we are 'bad' at a subject because we've been told so by others, or have come to believe it through initial failure. It is often the way that others see our ability that can make or break us. If we then set ourselves low standards, that's all we achieve. Your beliefs may well have affected your behaviour – bored reactions, demotivated listening, no positive participation or even disruption.

### Positive attitudes lead to positive behaviour

If we set ourselves high standards, we have a target to aim for. What is more this will actually help you **revise faster**!

*You can change the way you think about yourself. You can remove or unlearn barriers to your learning success and produce excellent results that you didn't believe you could!*

There is evidence that optimists (those who look on the bright side) cope better in life than pessimists (those who look on the dark side).

**Consider these points:**

**We learn approximately three times as slowly:**

- when we're bored, learning what seems to have no practical use
- what we don't like and what doesn't match our learning style and channel
- when we're anxious, stressed or we convince ourselves we can't do it
- in uncomfortable, unpleasant surroundings
- when we are tired, hungry or dehydrated
- when we feel negative and demotivated

*If you know **how** to learn, **what** you learn becomes much easier.*

**We learn fastest:**

- when we are relaxed, focused, motivated and positive
- using multisensory techniques and both Alpha and Beta brain waves
- in pleasant surroundings
- at a time that suits our body clock
- when we involve all our intelligences, especially our favourite and strongest ones
- when we **positively believe we can succeed**

### *So why is this important to you now?*

Have you ever used or heard the expression 'mind over matter'? We use it to explain how we overcame or succeeded in something by 'will power'.

Negative or worried thoughts cause our primitive brain to take control, and our ability to learn rapidly fades. Positive approaches increase learning; determinedly cheerful attitudes statistically produce the most successful people and the most successful results.

### *How can this knowledge help you now?*

Just by knowing that you possess the mind power to succeed, and by knowing that negative behaviour restricts clear, easy learning, you can begin to change your approach and learn to learn in a more stress-free manner. You open a motorway to your memory.

*The future's bright. The future's in your hands ...*

## How can I change my attitude?

- **Create a 'success dream'**
  This is a mental movie you 're-run' in your mind of an occasion when you've really succeeded at something. Dream it before you work – you'll feel much more positive.
- **Find a purpose**
  If you can think how or why something can be applied in 'real' life – why it will be useful, what purpose it has – then it will be easier to focus on with a positive attitude.
- **Discover determination and statements of intent**
  It's easy to tell someone to be determined, and much more difficult to achieve. One way is to list all the good intentions you have and place them on the wall of your study area. If you try to be positive, expect to work hard and intend to remember, it's amazing how you easily begin to memorise and attend to work.
- **Learn how to control stress and anxiety**
  Knowing how to calm down and work in a relaxed manner is an essential skill – look at pages 14–15.
- **Learn motivation**
  The self-discipline or 'get up and go' we all need – see page 12.
- **Boost your ego**
  Find someone who believes in you: perhaps a teacher or parent who understands what you are experiencing now. Positive feedback helps you feel good about yourself which is a great motivator.

# ★ Motivation

Motivation is a combination of your:

- inner drive and determination
- feeling able and ready to take on a task
- having a reason or purpose to do it

The good news is that it is possible to motivate yourself.

**Tick or highlight those that apply to you:**

| Demotivators | | Motivators | |
|---|---|---|---|
| Not understanding work | ❒ | Praise | ❒ |
| Poor marks | ❒ | Appreciation | ❒ |
| No praise for effort | ❒ | Reward | ❒ |
| Low confidence | ❒ | A plan that has worked | ❒ |
| Frustration with studies | ❒ | Steady improvement | ❒ |
| Lack of appreciation | ❒ | Successes, however small | ❒ |
| Slow or no progress | ❒ | Understanding from others | ❒ |
| Feeling overwhelmed | ❒ | Reassurances | ❒ |
| Leaving work until the last minute | ❒ | Higher marks | ❒ |
| Not feeling understood | ❒ | Enjoying a topic | ❒ |
| Feeling ignored | ❒ | Surprising yourself with greater effort | ❒ |
| | | A challenge | ❒ |
| | | Determination | ❒ |
| | | Small competitions | ❒ |
| | | Dreams of success in the future | ❒ |

Just understanding **how** you feel more motivated is a start!

## How can you motivate yourself?

- Look to the future – what sort of life do you want?
- Look for the purpose in your studies: 'If I do this, I will be able to . . .'
- Take pride in your work performance. Record **all** successes.
- Look back at previous success. Remember how you felt.
- Plan your work into a timetable – month, week and day.
- Break your topics down into manageable 'chunks'.
- Plan in your free-time activities.
- Set sensible time limits; it's not the number of hours you put in, it's how you use them.
- Find someone to help you understand.
- Talk to someone who knows what you're going through: any praise from them will motivate you.
- Praise yourself when you know you've got it right! Give yourself a reward!

Try them! You'll be surprised!

# Mind and body harmony

As you can tell from the previous pages, learning is not just about 'memorising'. It's about using the power of your brain, your mind and your body.

If you want to learn better, faster and more happily you should look after yourself. Do this by having a balanced diet, regular moderately intense exercise, at least eight hours sleep each night and by working in an environment you're comfortable with.

## ★ Fitness and Exercise

**Follow these important tips to help you improve:**

Exercise allows your body to work off tension, increase oxygen intake and improve your blood circulation, and gives your mind a break from study. Thirty minutes of moderately intense activity or walking hard or riding a bike for fifteen minutes five days a week will do. Fit it into your daily routine: it will bring health benefits, reducing stress and the possibility of illness as well as helping your positive thinking! Stretch, warm up – run, jog or walk. Try hand/eye co-ordination tasks such as juggling or throwing and catching. Swimming is especially good. When you have exercised hard, remember to 'warm down' to make sure your muscles are relaxed.

## ★ Feed your body, feed your brain!

Eating wisely creates energy and increases your chances of greater memory and less stress. A diet involving plenty of carbohydrates is preferable because they produce energy which will help you remember and learn better.

*Don't eat your evening meal too late. You need time to digest it before you sleep.*

***Here are some hints to help you eat for your results! Your diet should include:***

- fish, which is often known as 'brain food', is very good for you. It also helps keep your muscles fit
- food like bread, bagels, muffins and even malt loaf all include the necessary carbohydrates!
- plenty of fruit and vitamin C
- greens – these are packed with magnesium, which helps you cope with stress
- lean red meat or cereals and beans if you are a vegetarian – important sources of iron
- bananas – easily digested carbohydrates. Also a good source of potassium which is very important for stamina (low potassium often brings a feeling of confusion).
- water
- cereals – especially oats as they release a steady stream of carbohydrates during the day
- a light easily digestible lunch – perhaps pasta, salad and fruit

> ***Avoid*** *high sugar foods, artificial flavourings, fizzy drinks and too much tea or coffee when you are studying. All of these will stop you learning well!*

## ★ Create a happier environment

Your mind and your brain will function better if where you work is comfortable, safe, stress-free, well lit, of an average temperature, colourfully decorated and pleasing.

(See Part Two Motivation and your working environment, page 19.)

## ★ Sleep

*REM time makes up as much as 20% of our sleep.*

Relax before you go to sleep. Don't become overtired by forcing yourself to work late. Don't cut down on your optimum sleep time, that's about eight hours a night. Sleep is essential for keeping your brain in good condition for learning. The time known as rapid eye movement (REM) is when our brain sifts and sorts out information gained during the day. Your Theta brain waves are active at this time. These allow us to subconsciously solve problems, or discover answers to puzzling or difficult questions. So sleep time is **very** important to your relaxed and happy life.

> *You will tire quickly when revising – so proper sleep is essential.*

***If you don't sleep well try some of the following:***

- Exercise regularly, but not near bedtime
- Stick to regular bedtimes
- Allow some time to relax from your studies before going to bed
- Avoid caffeine near bedtime
- Listen to non-lyrical music
- Get up and do something monotonous

## ★ Wake up your brain!

Here are some things you can do to help make your brain much more receptive to learning and link both your hemispheres before each session. Because physical movement stimulates brain function, you will feel more relaxed and your negative feelings will drift away. This is another reason why exercise is so good for your learning.

### Go with the flow - drink $H_2O$

Drink plenty of pure water. It is a conductor of electricity and your brain functions with electrical impulses. A headache and tiredness can often be caused by dehydration and your learning will be very difficult and slow. Drink a glass of water for every 10 kilos of your weight per day: it heightens energy, improves concentration and helps your learning.

### Jump start your brain - to link both hemispheres

Your left hemisphere controls the right side of your body. Your right hemisphere controls the left side.

Stretch as if before playing sport – march on the spot moving your right arm with your left leg and vice versa. This will increase the blood and energy/electrical flow to the brain. Try drawing in mirror images with both hands, doodle identically with both hands or try juggling!

You will find that you can concentrate more immediately, that you can make quicker connections within your work and generally react faster mentally. This is because you have woken up both of your brain hemispheres.

### Release the stress

You can switch off panic before every revision session and in exams. Above your eyebrows, on your forehead, are two neurovascular points. As you panic blood rushes to the back of your head. By keeping your fingers pressed gently on these points, blood is encouraged to the front where your thinking takes place and you will be able to concentrate again. You can massage behind your ears to relieve stress too. If you rub and roll your earlobes you will listen and concentrate better! Some people do this subconsciously.

# ★ Managing stress

When you become anxious or worried your primitive brain seems to take control. This is what happens when you panic or go into shock. When this happens the rest of your brain slows down to slow motion, or 'freezes'.

So if you are unhappy, worried, annoyed, upset or frustrated, your ability to understand and remember is significantly harmed! This is called stress, and is a form of pressure. Everyone becomes stressed at one time or another, but if you

**recognise its cause**

**recognise its symptoms**

and **know how to handle it**

you will be able to cope much better. It's important to realise that you **can** control it.

## Causes of stress

There are a number of causes – and what stresses one person need not stress another. Look at the list below. Do you recognise any of them?

| | |
|---|---|
| Illness | Putting things off until the last minute |
| Being unfit | Failing to reach targets |
| A poor diet | Work mounting up |
| Low energy | Incompetence or imagined incompetence |
| People being annoying or demanding | Distractions |
| Peer group pressure | Interruptions |
| Bullying | Trying to do too much at once |
| Targets that are unrealistic | |

## Symptoms of stress

There are a number of recognised symptoms of stress. They can be:

### *Physical*

eating habits change (eating more/less) • too little or too much sleep • stomach disorders • nervous habits, fidgeting • headaches • cramps • muscle spasms • breathlessness • crying • clumsiness • violence • nausea • butterflies

### *Mental*

low self-confidence • guilty feelings • phobias and obsessions • loss of interest • lethargy • poor memory and concentration • failing to finish tasks • being irritable and angry • feeling lonely, isolated • hyperactivity • indecision • fearing the future

You may not experience all of these, but a combination of a few can be difficult to live with.

## How to handle stress

Firstly **recognise** you're stressed. Then try some or all of these:

| | |
|---|---|
| Exercise and fresh air | Try to predict the difficult times |
| Seek advice | Get enough sleep |
| Plan time | Talk positively to yourself |
| Plan in rewards and fun | Plan your goals and dream them! |
| Tense and then relax your muscles moving up from feet to face | Create a manageable daily routine |
| | Eat sensibly (see page 13) |

## Summary of Part One

# Brain Power!

To **immediately** learn better, to begin to revise successfully, you need to be aware of these essential parts of your **learning ability**:

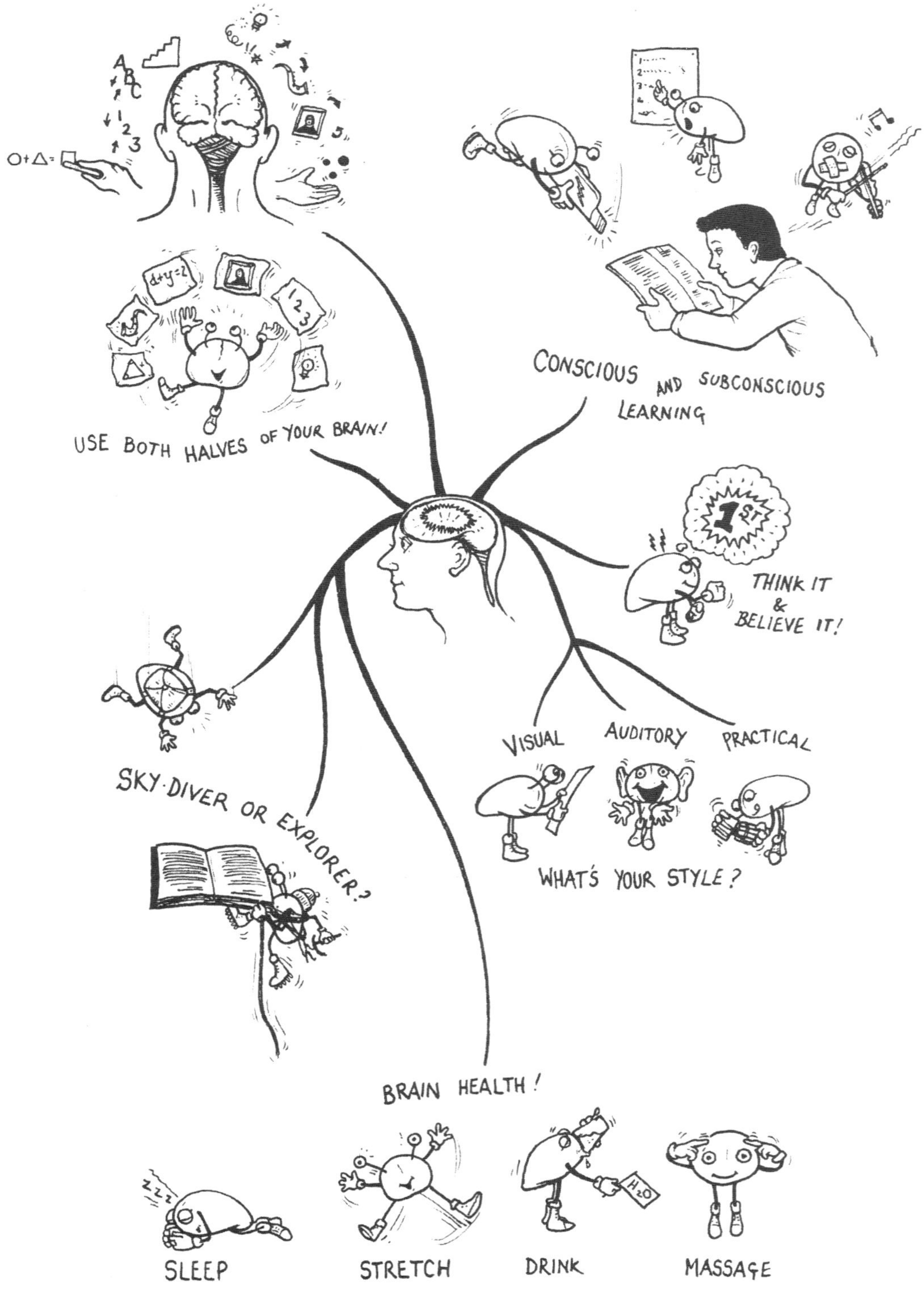

# Part 2
# Practical Revision Skills

*This section offers plenty of suggestions and skills that can be applied to any subject. These are explained in more detail in the range of* Longman Study Guides *listed on page 21. You can discover your **tailor-made** style, and learn to adapt and customise it to suit your subjects. There is also an action plan at the end of the book that will help you with your revision.*

# Your learning environment

## Equipment

The physical organisation of your workplace is very important. If you are to be relaxed and focused, your workplace must suit your purpose and you.

***What would you put in your environment to help you study?***

**Answer these questions, ticking the appropriate box:**

| I need ... | yes | no |
|---|---|---|
| a bed to study on | ❒ | ❒ |
| the right room temperature | ❒ | ❒ |
| lots of light | ❒ | ❒ |
| loud wordy music and TV | ❒ | ❒ |
| a roaring log fire (in winter of course!) | ❒ | ❒ |
| a deck-chair in the garden | ❒ | ❒ |
| a soft, comfy armchair | ❒ | ❒ |
| loads of interruptions from friends | ❒ | ❒ |
| all my books easily within reach | ❒ | ❒ |
| a good table and chair that match in height | ❒ | ❒ |
| chatty friends | ❒ | ❒ |
| water | ❒ | ❒ |
| posters | ❒ | ❒ |
| the correct texts and notes | ❒ | ❒ |
| a telephone | ❒ | ❒ |
| pens, pencils, boxes, folders, etc. | ❒ | ❒ |
| a computer, CD-ROMs and the Internet | ❒ | ❒ |
| a timetable and a list of topics to study | ❒ | ❒ |

*How you organise your room and furniture is very important – your workplace should be bright, comfortable, stimulating and inviting. After all, you'll use it a lot, so you need to feel safe in it and like it!*

***The 'kit' checklist***

**Your equipment**

pens, pencils, ruler
colours/highlighters, ink
corrector fluid/pen, rubber
filing dividers
folders/wallets/files
hole puncher, reinforcers
paper – plain, lined, graph, computer paper
index cards and box
personal organiser, diary, timetables
computer equipment, typewriter
music system
brain-boosting refreshments
calculator
paper clips, stapler
Blu-Tack, Sellotape
lamp, lighting
scissors
glue
dictaphone
dictionary, thesaurus
shelves, drawers
Post Its
pictures, posters

***Chasing equipment is a great time waster!***

**Recognise this?**

look for books – 10 minutes
check desk is tidy – 10 minutes
sharpen all pencils and put pens in colour co-ordinated pattern – 10 minutes
run around the house looking for more kit – 10 minutes
wonder where the time has gone; decide to take a break! – 2 minutes

## Motivation and your working environment

It is important that you surround yourself with things that make you feel positive and focused on success. In your work area these should be images and statements that will help motivate you. These will help stimulate you and remind you of your purpose and goals. For instance:

- photographs of people who are important to you and photographic records of previous 'successes'
- certificates and awards you have won
- newspaper clippings
- trophies, cups, mementoes
- positive comments, praise and recognition from others
- favourite posters/pictures that give you a good feeling
- motivational slogans. They don't necessarily suit everyone, but if they cheer you up, use them!

## Music and your working environment

*Too much tension inhibits learning – but too much relaxation can interfere with concentration.*

When you are engaged in hard, concentrated work your pulse and blood pressure tend to rise. Specific, carefully chosen music can really help you learn by creating a focused, alert, concentrated frame of mind. Remember you have a 'musical intelligence' that will help you learn faster!

Music to work by must be chosen carefully. It should preferably have about sixty beats a minute and be without words. Music like this awakens your creative right hemisphere – helping intuition, creative thought and subconscious working. It allows the academic left hemisphere to become involved in conscious learning at the same time. But if it distracts you when studying some topics or subjects, **don't** listen to it. You'll probably need to experiment with volume too – too loud and you'll lose concentration. It will take some time to learn what is best for you and may require some discipline and self-control.

Many people listen to classical music, such as baroque music (Vivaldi, Bach, Handel). You could also try 'Relax with the Classics' (LIND Institute) or Mendelssohn Violin Concertos 1 and 3. For something more contemporary try Enya's 'Watermark'.

*Avoid music that will dramatically slow down the brain's ability to learn, such as rave music.*

# ★ Resources

## Gathering resources effectively

Having all the information that is relevant at your disposal when you sit down to work is often more than half the battle.

Many students fail to realise that tracking down the sources of information on their topic and making a careful choice of which information to use will give them a greater knowledge of the subject. Using lots of different resources will make your learning really **multisensory**!

**Typical resources include:**

| | |
|---|---|
| books – reference and text | photocopies and class notes |
| catalogues | newspapers |
| videos | slides/photographs |
| TV/radio | audio tapes |
| encyclopaedias | libraries and librarians |
| places | |

And don't forget:

**people** – don't ignore them; the information they have is: personal, real, immediate, informative, often interesting and normally free! But make sure they know what they're on about!

**computers** – information technology, e.g. CD-ROM and the Internet. The Worldwide web is a source of information so exploit it if you can. These resources are often very easy to use because the instructions and skills are interactive. (But be warned, they are also potentially distractive too!)

***Can you think of any more?***

## How should you use your resources?

If you favour the **visual 'whole picture' learning channel** you may want to get an overview by watching a video before researching specific facts from books.

If you favour the **step-by-step auditory learning channel** you may want to interview people and put the pieces together yourself.

If you favour the **practical learning channel** you may prefer to visit museums, experience real-life situations or try the 'hands on' approach.

*Make sure you combine all strategies and use a variety of different resources.*

**You should:**

- plan your time
- rank your resources in order of importance
- overview your resources and to begin with pick one that gives you a general understanding
- learn to skim and scan read. You could use highlighters or underline if the text belongs to you.
- make simple notes from each new resource. Don't forget to leave space, use colours and patterns to help you memorise as you go along.
- use a tape recorder or a camera if appropriate
- make a reference: a note of your source (this will save time if you need to refer back to the source)

## ★ Really useful equipment

There are many study aids available to help you with subject-specific study and revision.

Try ***Longman Study Guides***, which offer you help and guidance throughout your GCSE course. Written by Examiners, these books will help you to fully understand the topics you are covering at school, and will provide you with study and revision advice, and exam practice.

***Longman Exam Practice Kits*** can be used at any time, but are particularly useful in the second year of your course. Examiners briefly explain the essential parts of each topic, and then provide examination questions for you to try. There are also some complete examination papers to work through, with answers and advice.

***Longman Practice Exam Papers*** are ideal for use prior to your mock exams and the actual exams. Consisting of complete examination papers, you are encouraged to work through them in exam-like conditions. Answers are provided, and the Examiner gives lots of tips and hints to help you make sure that you gain maximum marks.

***The Longman study aids range is available from good bookshops.***

# Organising time and mind

Managing your time helps you to do the things that **need** to be done, **when** they need to be done, in the **way** they need to be done! It takes a small investment in time to learn how to do this – and it saves you hours!

When you are revising, how you use your time is very important. If you don't take care you'll find you waste your own time. What isn't achieved in one day is passed over into the next and you start having to use your 'free' time to catch up. This only causes you to feel downhearted, as if you are making no progress.

Time management helps you keep in control and keeps your attitude positive. It is a skill that is as important as memory techniques and exam skills!

| | |
|---|---|
| Estimate how much time you spend actually working each day throughout the week | **Total for the week** ____________ |
| How much time do you spend asleep (officially!), eating, travelling and in generally maintaining yourself? | **Total for the week** ____________ |
| Add these two totals together | **Total** ____________ |
| Now deduct the work and maintaining time from 168 (the number of hours in a week)<br>How much free time do you have? | **Total for the week** ____________ |

How is that time split up each day? Are you wasting your own time?

**Are any of these familiar? Tick those that are ✓**

- ❐ Sleep
- ❐ Work
- ❐ Late work
- ❐ Re-done work
- ❐ Sport
- ❐ Art
- ❐ Music
- ❐ Hobbies/activities
- ❐ Interruptions
- ❐ Helping others
- ❐ Distractions
- ❐ Chatting
- ❐ Illness
- ❐ Duties and responsibilities
- ❐ Last minute research
- ❐ Poor planning
- ❐ Travel
- ❐ Not listening in class
- ❐ Visits
- ❐ Problems
- ❐ Worry
- ❐ Poor motivation/self-discipline

Some will be under your control and some won't. Highlight those that are!

# ★ A guide to planning your time

**Easy to understand instructions!**

**1** Take a piece of paper. Write down your timetable each week – analyse your:

**work time** (lessons, homework);
**maintenance time** (sleep, wash, rest, travel, etc.);
**free time** (portion per day, i.e. ÷ 7).

**2** Write down 'What wastes my time'

**3** Work out your **targets**
(aims, objectives ... what you've got to do!) for the forthcoming:
week
month
year
in order of importance,
i.e. **vital**!
**delay it**!
**forget it**!

**4** Put them into your timetable, diary or personal organiser

**5** Make sure to do the **top priority** ones first:
As – **do it**
Bs – **delay it** (what you can do later)
Cs – **drop it** (what you don't **have** to do)

**6** Make sure you **stick to your plan**
(lots of students spend hours drawing 'state of the art' plans and timetables ... and then neglect them)

**Benefits?**

- you're on time
- you're less stressed
- last minute panics are less likely
- you'll have more **free** time
- you'll see how you can improve
- you'll see how you study best
- you'll feel good!

**and**

- ... you'll make progress!

# ★ Revision timetables

*Unfortunately, few students know how to put a really effective revision timetable together.*

A timetable to help you revise is as important as any other skill, perhaps more so.

With a timetable you will be able to plan in every topic and reassure yourself that you can fit in all the work. The timetable will also help you plan to work at a time when you know you work your best. You will be able to plan in a **memory review** programme which ensures that you cover everything in enough detail and that you repeat it often enough and in a variety of ways. You will be able to keep a record of your progress and mark in areas that are in need of help or further emphasis. You will be able to plan in your free time activities that are so vital for motivation and relaxation. You will also be able to plan in your rewards for your achievements. In addition you will be able to show others how you are coping and find both support and encouragement from this.

- You should have a **long-term timetable**. This is best done as an overview of each month. You can mark on it everything you have to do including which subjects you intend to revise on which day.
- You should have a list of all topics for each subject (see your teacher – and don't leave any out).
- You should identify those topics you know best and prioritise the others.
- You should also have a **weekly** timetable – mark on it when you intend to revise, work normally and relax: fill in your topics for each day.
- You should build in a 5 minute review time each evening for each topic, and the same the following morning. At the end of each week you should again review each topic for a few minutes. This will keep your memory and familiarity of a topic topped up.
- You should tick each topic when you have revised it – and you should review each topic at least three times in detail.
- You should build in **spare time**: a period each day. This is 'flexitime', when you can catch up or relax if you've done well.

## Review pattern

### *Reinforcing your learning*

Below you can see how much time you can save by building regular reviewing time into your timetable. This means creating a timetable that includes time to go over a topic briefly at the end of the day. Allow time to go over it again for just a few minutes before starting your revision session the following morning.

*We forget 70% of what we learn within 24 hours if we don't repeat it!*

If you revise a topic and then ignore it for three weeks, you will have to start the whole process again. You could be wasting as much as 50% of your time and effort! Look at the illustration below:

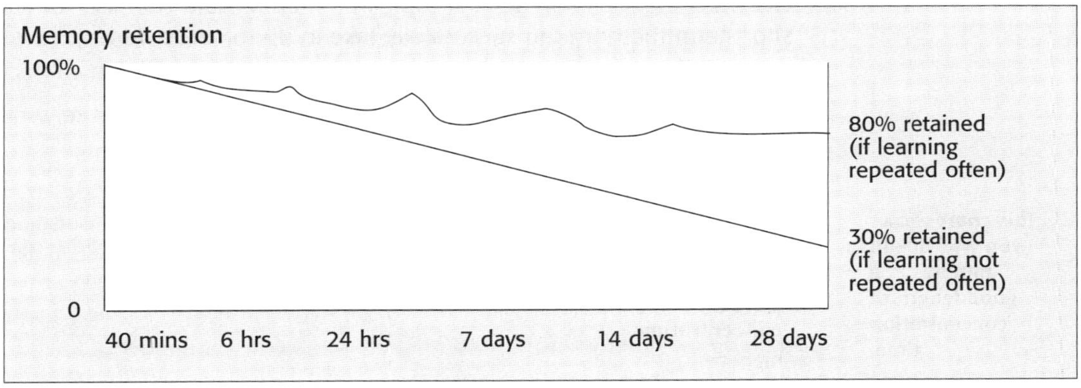


*If you review regularly, you will increase how much you remember with less effort.*

## Cramming

Cramming means doing most of your studying in one big block of time, just before your exam. You cram it into your head. There are a number of reasons why this is unwise:

- it goes in fast and out fast. It takes time to revise properly – look at the chart above!
- it causes exam fatigue. You're tired before you start, you may give your best in the first two or three exams, but then you slow down. This puts you under stress and damages your results.
- when you cram you don't have an overview. Long-term learning, a little and often, gives you the big picture.

### *When is cramming OK?*

It is acceptable when you have been using a review timetable and you need to fill a **few** gaps. Cramming in this instance would be better called 'last-minute filling'!

*It's not the number of hours you put in – it's how you use those hours!*

# Revision sessions

## Quick guide to maximum success

You should think about the following areas before you sit down to study:

### Session Planning

- Choose your topic from your timetable.
- Plan sessions of no more than 30–40 minutes for revision and plan a 5 to 10 minute break at the end of each session.
- Overview the topic. Break your topic into manageable chunks – of about seven parts. (Our short-term memory can successfully take in up to seven items.)
- Allocate time to your topic main headings.
- Decide on the various methods you think will help – read, recite, write, draw, highlight.
- Plan a reward: something to look forward to – activity/pastime.

**This chart shows you why 30–40 minutes is a good length of concentration time.**

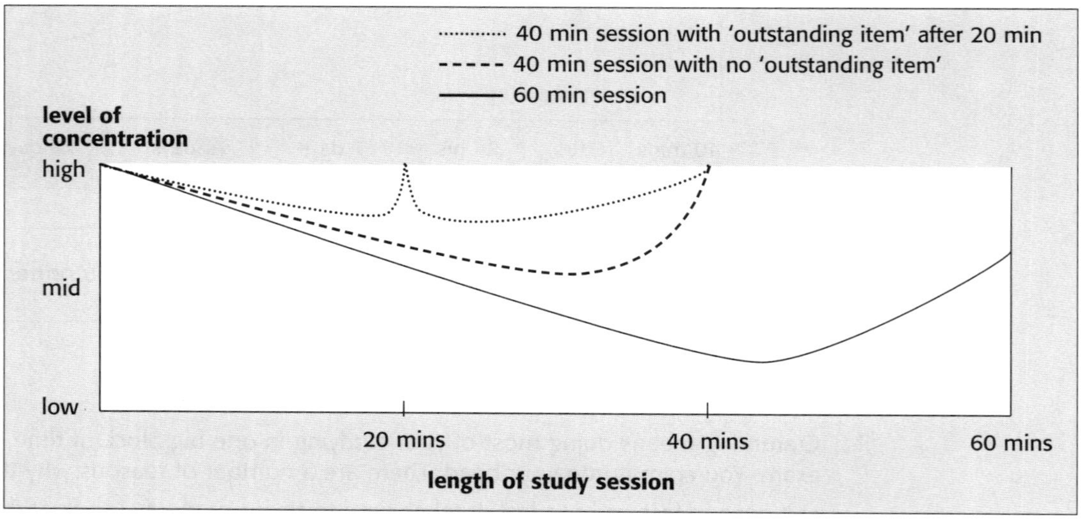


Try to have a mini-break – this is often called an 'outstanding item'. Use this time to draw a picture or diagram; take an overview – anything that relates to the subject but changes the way you're working for a few minutes. It refreshes you.

*Don't martyr yourself by studying for hours without breaks – it's the quality of work not the number of hours that counts!*

### Work area

- Should be peaceful, perhaps with non-lyrical music playing.
- You need good light, both natural and artificial.
- Make sure you are comfortable.
- Have all equipment ready – especially your notes, questions and past papers and your session plan.

### Brain motivation

- Fix on your purpose and intend to work!
- Relax.
- Be positive and put yourself in a winning attitude.
- Talk with someone who is reassuring and supportive before you start your session.

## Multisense your work

- Drink water and do some brain exercises to link both hemispheres.
- We remember 20% of what we see, 30% of what we say, 40% of what we hear, 50% of what we do … **and over 80% of what we see, hear, say and do!** Choose wisely! Choose a revision strategy that involves all your senses!
- If you are attempting a past paper, use all the techniques you have been taught. Don't forget to stick to the actual timing.
- Overview the topic and then study each part in depth.
- Half-way through each session include an outstanding item (see concentration span chart).
- At the end of each session take a few minutes to stretch and brain exercise.

## As you work

- Ask yourself questions about the topic: 'What do I really need to do?' 'Who, why, what, when, where, how?'.
- Look for obvious links and comparisons.
- Occasionally move and stretch.
- Alter your multisensory method to add variety. It will heighten concentration and increase memory.
- If you daydream, dream quickly so you can return to the matter at hand.

## At the end of your session

- At the end, review your work for 5 minutes, **remember to go over it again within 24 hours**.
- Ask yourself, 'What have I achieved? What was difficult? How can I tackle it better next time? Who can I ask for help?'
  Note your progress in your diary/organiser.
- **Go and have a good break** (at least 10 minutes if you are planning to move on to a new topic immediately).

***By making sure your learning and revision are active you will retain much more information.***

**Active learners are:**

**Those who**

are in control of time
concentrate on key points/facts
use multisensory methods
apply the skills and knowledge they've gained to many situations
set priorities
find a purpose to motivate them
prepare and plan ahead
are inquisitive
brainstorm (scribble down all thoughts on the subject to help create links and find answers)
record progress
discuss work with others
take notes well, using space and colour to help them memorise
can identify and interpret key questions

## ★ Revising with others

Working in pairs or in small groups can be very useful and successful because it involves your auditory memory and interpersonal intelligence. You are very involved in an active way and it often helps you gain greater understanding and enables you to explain a topic or point more clearly.

*Groupwork can help you revise faster, use more than one person's brain to learn something, and memorise by telling and asking.*

**But** it is important to choose your group (two or three is about right) very carefully and agree a **contract**. This is a set of study rules which will help you gain the full benefit from working with others.

*If you learn to work together, you can learn even faster.*

The contract you draw up should help you make sure that:

- you set a time limit on your study sessions (a maximum of 30 minutes)
- you agree **what** is to be studied and who does what
- you divide the work evenly
- all involved are enabled to take part equally
- a record is kept of what is said and achieved
- everyone takes responsibility
- all suggestions are listened to
- criticism is positive

**There are many benefits to be gained from groupwork:**

- you gain a sense of 'teamwork' and achievement
- it's more enjoyable
- you get further suggestions, tips, techniques
- other peoples' views
- you share your effort and time and so you are even more motivated

**And there are also some dangers:**

- it can distract you
- you may choose the wrong partner
- you may do all the work!
- if you fail to agree a plan or 'rules' to work by, the session may turn into a free-for-all!

*Don't allow the session to develop into a social chat!*

# Memory skills

## Learning and remembering

All learning depends upon memory – without it **everything** we did would be a new experience. **Constant repetition is vital.**

> *You know that 70% of what we learn today is gone within 24 hours unless you **intend** to remember it and **review** it.*

### How does the memory work?

*Think of a chart video you have seen and know well – how did your brain learn it so well without you realising?*

You have a 'working' or **short-term** memory. It's the holding centre for about a maximum of seven pieces of information at any one time.

You have a **long-term** memory, a permanent 'filing cabinet'.

Your working memory receives information through your senses. If you see it, say it, hear it and do it in a revision session you will create a four-lane motorway into your long-term memory. This is why you should learn in a **multisensory** way and use them all to make as many different connections as you can. So sitting for hours and just reading will take you four times as long to memorise the same information!

If the information is not rehearsed it will be lost or replaced by new information within seconds.

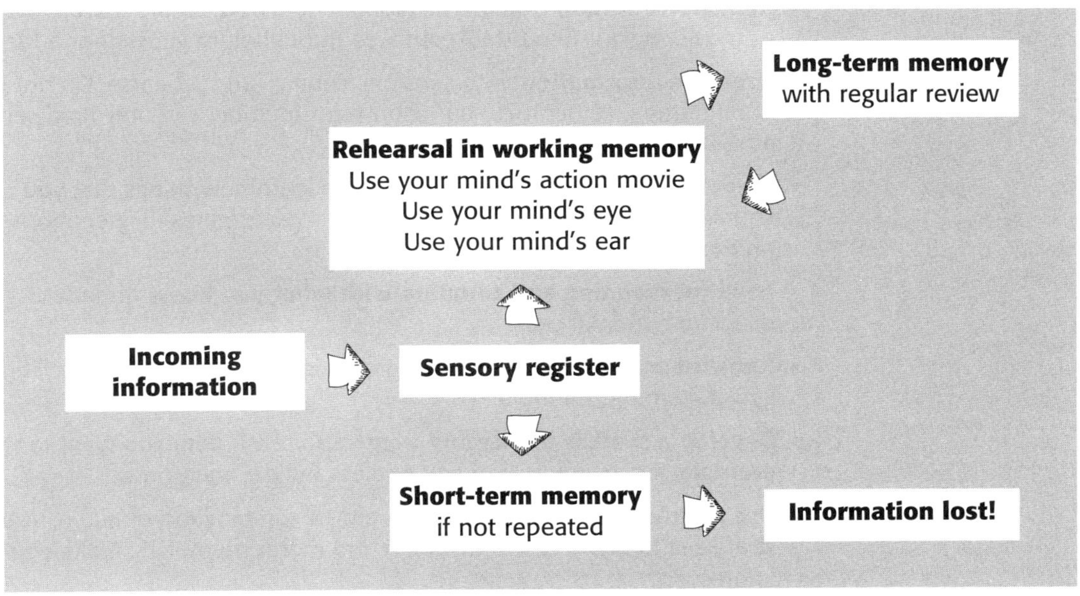


### Why do we forget?

1. Poor understanding
2. Poor attention, poor listening
3. Distractions
4. Your physical state – tiredness, anxiety, emotions, mood and stress
5. Interference – new information being confused with existing information (e.g. French Revolution followed by Russian Revolution)
6. Poor learning strategy – not having cues or memory triggers to unlock and retrieve the facts
7. Disuse or insufficient rehearsal or practice using a review cycle
8. Lack of importance – you don't remember the unimportant
9. Improper organisation – trying to cram too much information into your memory without sorting it into categories
10. Dehydration – the brain needs lots of water to conduct electrical pulses fast

## How we remember

***Use learning strategies***

Mnemonics – using the initial letters to create a sentence – Richard Of York Gave Battle In Vain = Red Orange Yellow Green Blue Indigo Violet (colours of the rainbow)

Rhyming poem – Thirty Days hath September ...

Chant, make up a song rap

Look, cover, write, say, check (repeat and test)

Locations or room system – assign places/objects around your room to key facts. **Visualise** the room and the facts return too!

Number rhymes – for example: 1 = bun, 2 = shoe, 3 = tree, 4 = door ... By using words that rhyme with the numbers, make up a silly phrase that helps you remember numbers or dates.

## Techniques to aid memory

- **Create interest**: find a purpose, 'This is useful because ...'
- **Understand it**: it's impossible to learn what you don't understand.
- **Positive thinking and confidence**: sometimes we fail to learn because we have convinced ourselves we can't do it.
- **Intend to attend to it!** Be determined to learn – avoid distractions.
- **Rehearse out loud**: speak the information aloud; create a script; verbalise. Create a story or movie in your mind (talk your way through it, to yourself or a friend).
- **Organise information**: into sensible 'chunks' and rehearse. Do not try to learn too much at one time – remember your short-term memory can only hold seven items. Plan in advance what you are going to tackle.
- **Create associations**: it's much easier to learn new things that you can link to something you already know (e.g. carbon dioxide → car engines → greenhouse effect → trees → photosynthesis → carbon dioxide).
- **Look for meaning and compare with what you know already**: e.g. how do plant cells differ from animal cells?
- **Remember the 'unusual'**: if something is funny, strange, spooky, bizarre or even if it's vulgar it's more memorable!
- **Develop a system of memory triggers** for each item you want to remember. For example, a souvenir will trigger endless holiday memories.
- **Use a multisensory approach**: employ a combination of audio, visual and physical strategies to use your visual, audio and motor memories. Make your facts varied and interesting.
- **Be relaxed**: play non-lyrical music to help the Alpha waves buzz.
- **Doodle, highlight, cartoon, underline**: use colour, charts, diagrams, drawings, brain-frames, flash cards, posters. Hang them round your room to aid **subconscious learning**. Record ideas and listen when you are relaxing. Make key ideas and facts stand out.
- **Involve your emotions**: you will find it easier to remember things that make you feel happy, amused, successful and praised.
- **You remember best the information you receive at the beginning and end of a work session**. Try having a very short change in the middle of a work session to create a false ending and beginning to give your memory a boost. Study for a maximum of 30–40 minutes, then break.
- **Use concrete materials**: make a model or a game to represent the information you need to remember.

### *The power of visualisation*

Visualisation is a process by which you can make a word or story come alive in your head by experiencing it or 'living' it with all your senses. It's a mental movie.

Have a look at the following example:

**The sensations you experience at a fun fair**

Hear the crowds and music

Feel the wind as you go on a ride

Experience the jolts and speed

See the colours, the people and the rides

Taste the candyfloss

Feel the happy atmosphere and excitement

Hear the screams of fear and enthusiasm!

Smell the hotdogs...

**How to learn something new**

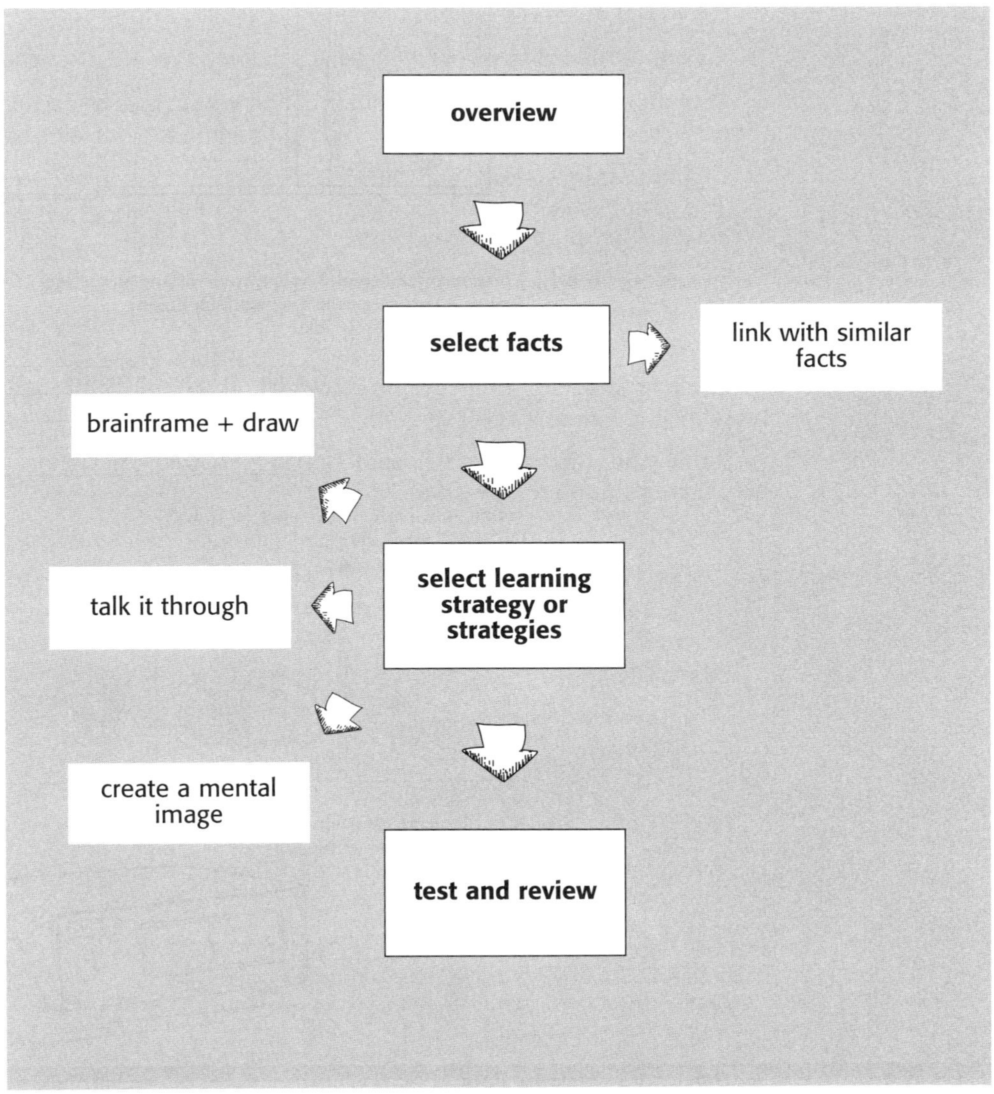

# ★ Examples

An exercise using multisensory memory skills taken from a *Longman Study Guide.*

**Extract I** *Vous êtes chez votre correspondante française, Janine. Janine vous montre la maison.*

1 Indiquez la salle à manger sur le plan (avec un X). *(1)*

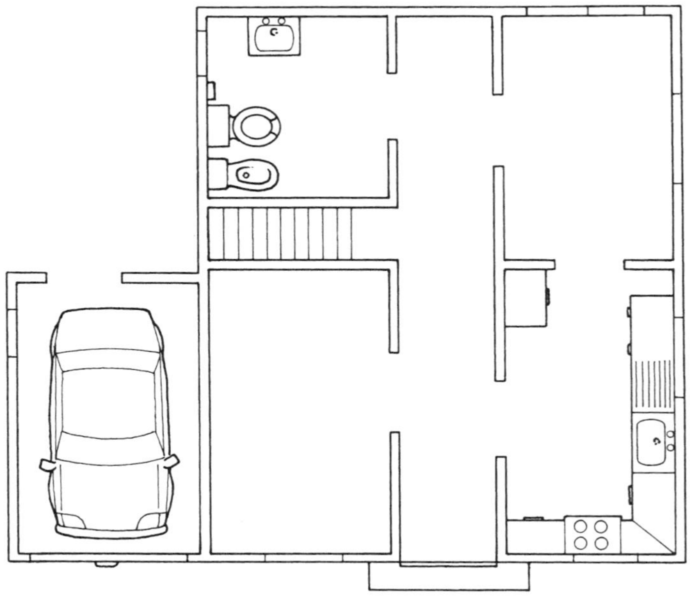

2 Vous regardez l'emploi du temps de Janine au collège.
Janine, qu'est-ce qu'elle a le vendredi matin?
Remplissez les cases vides.

| jeudi | | vendredi | |
|---|---|---|---|
| 9h | Anglais | 9h | |
| 10h | Sciences | 10h | Histoire |
| 11h | Français | 11h | |

*(2)*

3 Janine vous parle du déjeuner au collège.
Qu'est-ce que c'est?
Cochez la bonne case. *(1)*

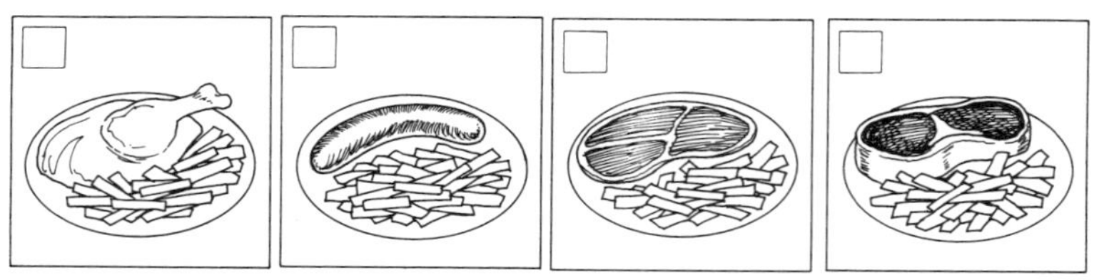

4 A quelle heure est-ce que vous allez manger?
Ecrivez l'heure en chiffres. *(1)*

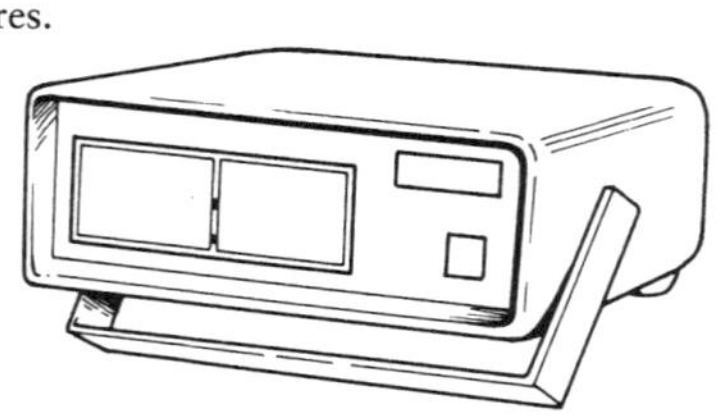

**Taken from *Longman Study Guide: GCSE French*, pp. 74–5**

# Reading and learning

It's vital to be able to read according to your need so that you are able to gain the best information in the shortest possible time. The most important aspect of reading at GCSE is understanding, and it may well be possible to achieve this without having to read every word.

> *A good student will be able to vary **how** they read according to **why** they have to read it.*

At GCSE you have to read for the following reasons:

- For practical reasons – instructions and so on (understanding).
- For general information (general impression – skim through).
- For specific information (fact finding – in-depth study).
- To learn and memorise (understanding and revision).
- To criticise (making up your own mind).
- To detect bias (is the passage one-sided?).

***Always plan before you start:***

Why should I have to read this?

How should I start?

What am I looking for?

Therefore what sort of reading do I need?

***There are three main ways to read that will help you:***

**Skimming:** This is gaining a general impression of what the chapter/book is mainly about.

**Scanning:** This is fact finding – looking for specific detail by running your eye down a page fast.

**Detailed reading:** This is reading for understanding: information, comprehension, detecting bias and to extract detailed answers.

# ★ Improve your reading techniques

## Understanding memory and speed

1. You must be **committed and willing** to improve your reading.
2. It always helps to get an **overview** first.
3. **Comprehension** is more important than speed.
   (250–400 wpm = good. 500+ wpm = excellent. 1000 wpm = you're a liar!)
4. Don't follow words **individually**, but in groups. Use punctuation to help.
5. If you want to increase your reading speed, try not to mouth words as you read. (We read four times slower this way.)
6. **Avoid back-tracking** – when your eyes flick back and re-read subconsciously. Following the text with a ruler or your finger will stop you if this is a real problem for you.
7. Using a guide (ruler or finger) can also help you train yourself to read faster . . . but keep it moving.
8. It can help to use **coloured transparent plastic** sheets (purple or yellow) over the text to stop the words jumping or glaring.
9. **Constant practice is vital** (you'll **understand** more, maybe even faster).
10. **Make notes** or use a highlighter – the physical activity helps link right and left hemispheres and improves understanding.

## SSQ3R

When reading in a memory/revision session you should use a strategy known as SSQ3R:

| | | |
|---|---|---|
| S | Skim | Check title and contents. Take a fast look at the pages to get a feel for the text. Look at the chapter headings, sections, illustrations and diagrams. |
| S | Scan | Look at the index. Fast-moving reading; eyes flicking across the page for key words/phrases. |
| Q | Question | Ask yourself your purpose; what do I want to know? Do I want to read it all? |
| R | Read | In depth. Find the speed at which you best understand. Try to familiarise yourself with specialist vocabulary. |
| R | Recall | Check understanding. Underline/highlight. Take notes. Test yourself. Have you fully answered the questions; is the argument clear? |
| R | Review | How have you done? What have you learnt? How can you improve? Identify and concentrate on your weak areas. |

The skills of smarter reading will help you:

- save yourself time
- increase your understanding
- increase your reading speed
- be able to sift through information better and faster
- increase your memory
- understand questions and themes more easily
- plan your work and answers better
- feel more in control!

# Listening skills

There's a difference between **listening** – information is processed by the conscious brain and is remembered – and **hearing** – when information is not processed but discarded unless it is relevant.

*The better you listen, the smarter you'll be.*

*By listening better you can save yourself hours later on.*

***Did you know . . . ?***

- We listen in spurts and we think four times faster than anyone can talk; our attention wanders every 30 seconds or so.
- We often hear what we expect to hear.
- We don't listen effectively when we are doing other things.
- We listen better when we are actively involved; asking questions, taking notes.
- If we have a good reason for listening, we listen accurately.

**Here's a mnemonic to help you remember**

*We always hear but we don't often listen!*

| | |
|---|---|
| **L** Link and locate | On your way to your lesson try to anticipate what you'll be studying. Make yourself mentally prepared – in the right frame of mind. |
| **I** Indicators | Listen for the two to three themes or objectives that the teacher will introduce early – the main ideas of the lesson/topic. |
| **S** Selective words | These are key selected words to listen for: 'It is vital that . . .' 'There are three reasons why . . .' 'You should consider . . .' Teachers will also signal these with gestures, pauses and so on. |
| **T** Try 'body language' | You can be an active and silent listener. It's called body language. Be on time. Sit where you can be seen. Join in. Show interest. Your positive body language helps the teacher teach better! |
| **E** Enquire | Ask questions – they clear up any misunderstandings and help you remember what you hear. |
| **N** Notes | Taking notes is an easy way of concentrating and remembering what you hear. There are many methods; see the next section for advice on note taking. |

# Note taking

Do you know why note taking is vital?

Note taking and making is one of **the** most important revision skills you need because:

1. It's active. It involves concentration.
2. Your memory likes simple notes in a spacious area.
3. It acts as a permanent trigger for your longer notes, essays and answers.
4. You automatically link both sides of your brain when you're taking notes – and double your learning speed!

***How's your note taking?***

**Tick or highlight those which apply to you**

| **Do you:** | **Yes** | **No** |
|---|---|---|
| never take notes? | ❐ | ❐ |
| fail to plan notes? | ❐ | ❐ |
| copy too much detail? | ❐ | ❐ |
| waste time rewriting again? | ❐ | ❐ |
| cram everything on to one page? | ❐ | ❐ |
| ignore layout and presentation? | ❐ | ❐ |
| ever use abbreviations? | ❐ | ❐ |
| ever use colour? | ❐ | ❐ |

## Different types of notes

**Linear notes:**

These are notes written in lines, often in lists and as 'bullet points'. You can 'number' each point in a variety of ways – but be consistent within each list. This is an example:

**STEP 1**
- i Think before you start – key words/facts/ideas only
- ii Use label and title symbols

**STEP 2**
- i Layout/shape/space
- ii Underline – central idea
- iii Diagrams/illustrations: visual = easy to learn
- iv Shorthand/abbreviations
- v Colour: memories like colour!
- vi Headings and numbers

**STEP 3**
- i Link points
- ii Arrows/circles/boxes
- iii Add in later: quotes; opinions

**Diagrams:**

These are also called mind networking/brain patterns/spidergrams/patterned notes/brainframes!

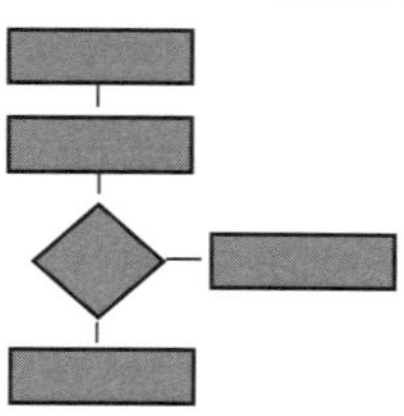
flow chart

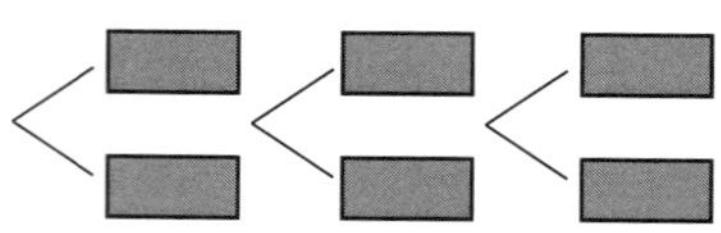
fishbone

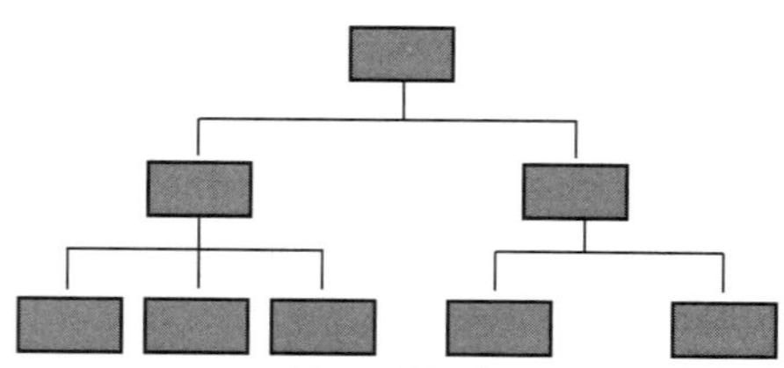
hierarchical

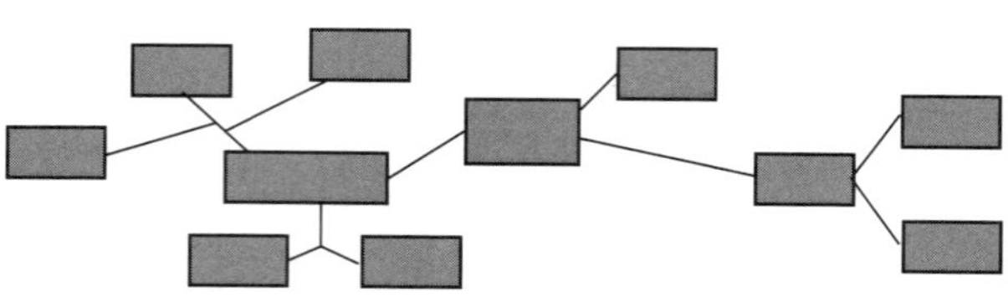
learning maps

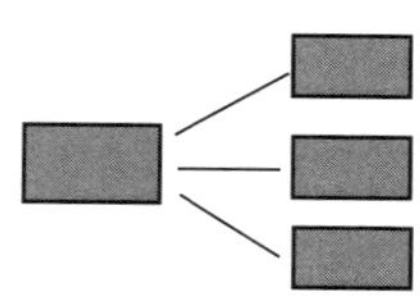
spray notes

***How to make spidergrams or brainframes***

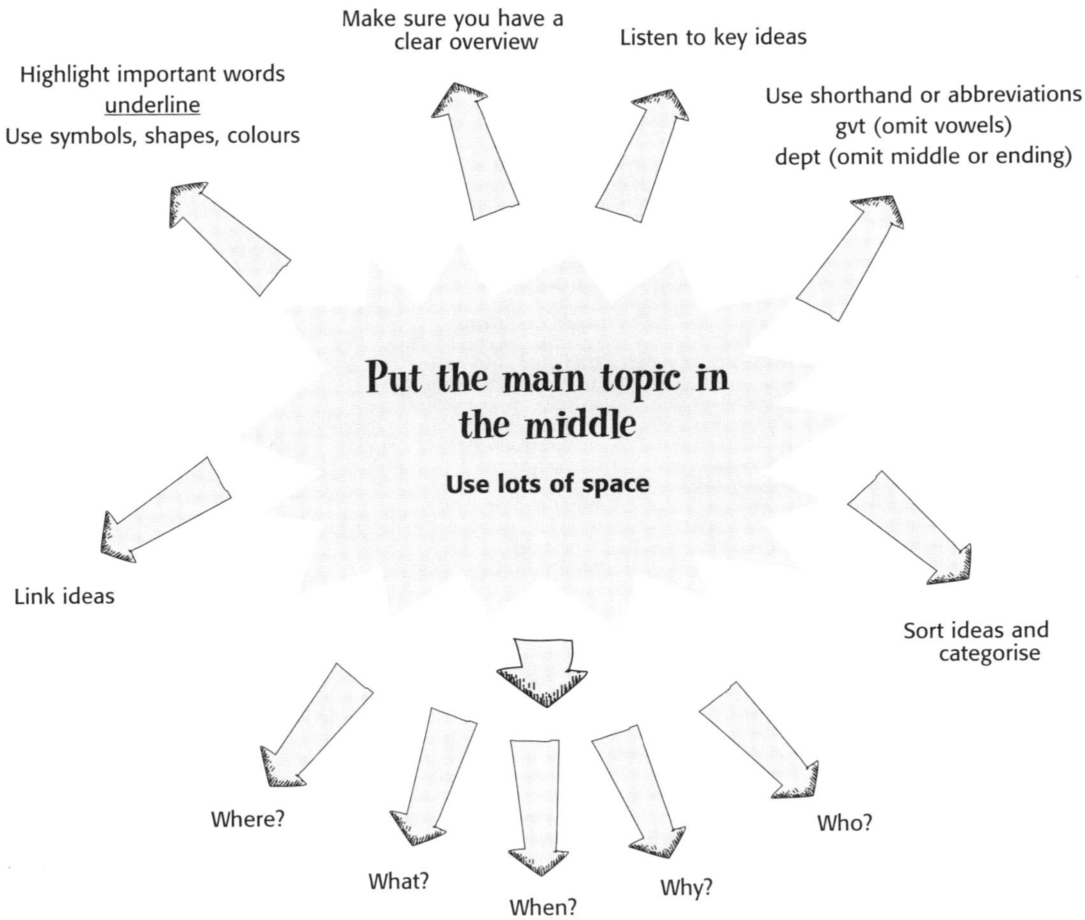


## Try developing and using symbols

- Use a 'dash' when you have to leave a word out
- Keep a wide margin
- Use a new line or branch for each new point

**Try your own shorthand. Can you translate these?**

| | |
|---|---|
| @ | // |
| &(+) | → |
| + | Ω |
| > | *c.* |
| < | ≠ |
| = | *pp* |
| % | *viz* |
| *C20th* | *ms* |
| ∴ | ≈ |
| | *ff* |

**Different kinds of emphasis**

boxing

CAPITALS

**bold**

highlight

underline

**A numbering and lettering system to try**

- I, II, III, = main headings, then i, ii, iii
- A, B, C = points below main heading, then a, b, c
- 1, 2, 3 = less important

It's important to find your information easily so you need to:

- file notes systematically
- have a contents page
- have dividers and new files where necessary
- label/number clearly
- keep all files in one place
- keep notes neat: re-file occasionally

# ★ Examples

Some of the different forms of note taking that you might use, taken from *Longman Study Guides*.

## Linear notes

Suppose that you were researching the following topic: 'Acting in the Seventeenth-Century Theatre'. After a period of thinking, discussion and general reading you may make two lists along these lines:

*What I know already*

(a) Some seventeenth-century actors are famous, e.g. Richard Burbage, Edward Alleyn, Shakespeare himself.
(b) Boys played women's parts.
(c) Stages were often in the open.
(d) There were few costumes and props.
(e) Audiences were from a wide cross-section of the public.
(f) Puritans were opposed to the theatres and players.

*What I need to find out*

(a) What evidence is available of early theatres and players? Is there much good source material?
(b) Were there theatres outside London?
(c) Which were the most popular plays and players?
(d) What status did acting have as a profession?
(e) Why were the Puritans so hostile to theatres and acting?

In contrast, consider a contemporary topic: 'Drug-Taking as a Threat to Young People Today'. Possibly, after thinking, discussing and reading, your lists of ideas might look something like this:

*What I know already*

(a) There are TV films and videos warning young people against drugs.
(b) Some young people have been prosecuted for drug-handling.
(c) People in the news sometimes set a bad example to the young.
(d) Drugs can kill.
(e) Some dangerous drugs are fairly easily obtained.
(f) Drug-taking can lead to crime to finance the habit.
(g) Some powerful drugs are used as medicines.

*What I need to find out*

(a) What organizations help and advise young people about drug-taking?
(b) What laws are there about obtaining and using drugs?
(c) What proportion of young people today take drugs?
(d) How much money does the average drug-taker spend on the habit?
(e) What are the names of the dangerous drugs?
(f) What cures are there for drug dependency?

**Taken from *Longman Study Guide: GCSE English*, pp. 68–69**

## Topic trees and flowcharts

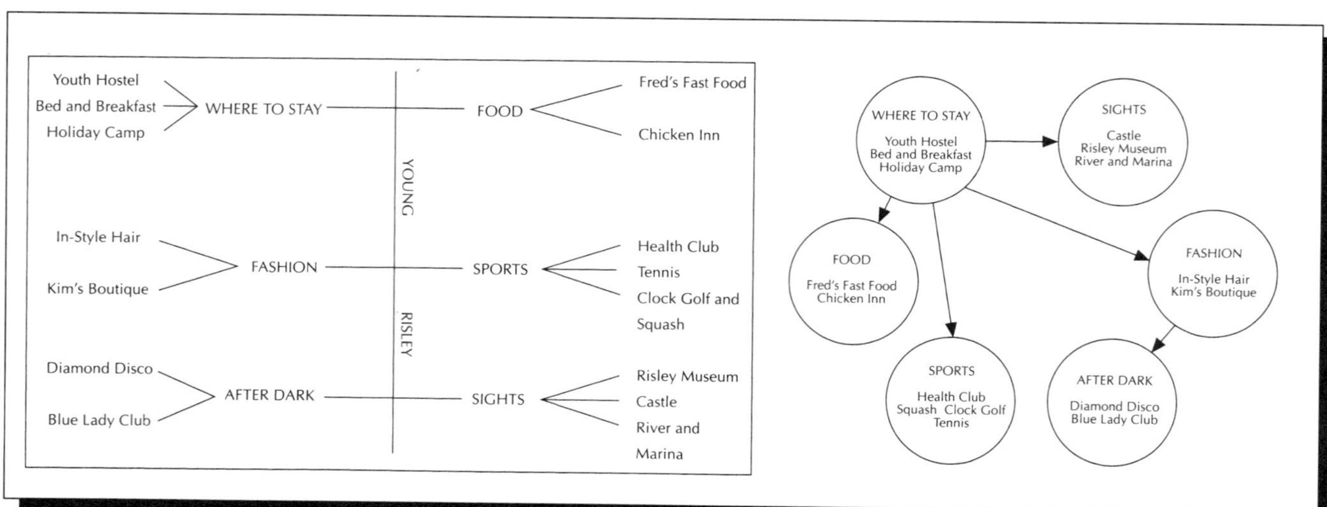


**Taken from *Longman Study Guide: GCSE English*, p. 135**

# Written answers

## Some general tips

This section deals with the skills that will help you in your written assignments whether you are preparing coursework, revising, practising past papers or coping with the actual answers in an exam. These include:

- a section setting out the principles of written assignments by using the mnemonic: ESSAY
- typical command words you will find in GCSE questions as well as words you can use to signpost or signal your answer more clearly in an exam
- a number of examples of written assignments from the *Longman Study Guides*. For more precise subject information you should consult these books, the information given by exam boards, and your teachers who are taking you through the actual syllabus.

*Essays, paragraph answers, writing in prose are all a **problem solving process**.*

Below are the steps required in any written assignment; all questions, essays and assignments are problems that need to be solved. The diagram shows the steps you need to go through to reach a conclusion or solution to a question.

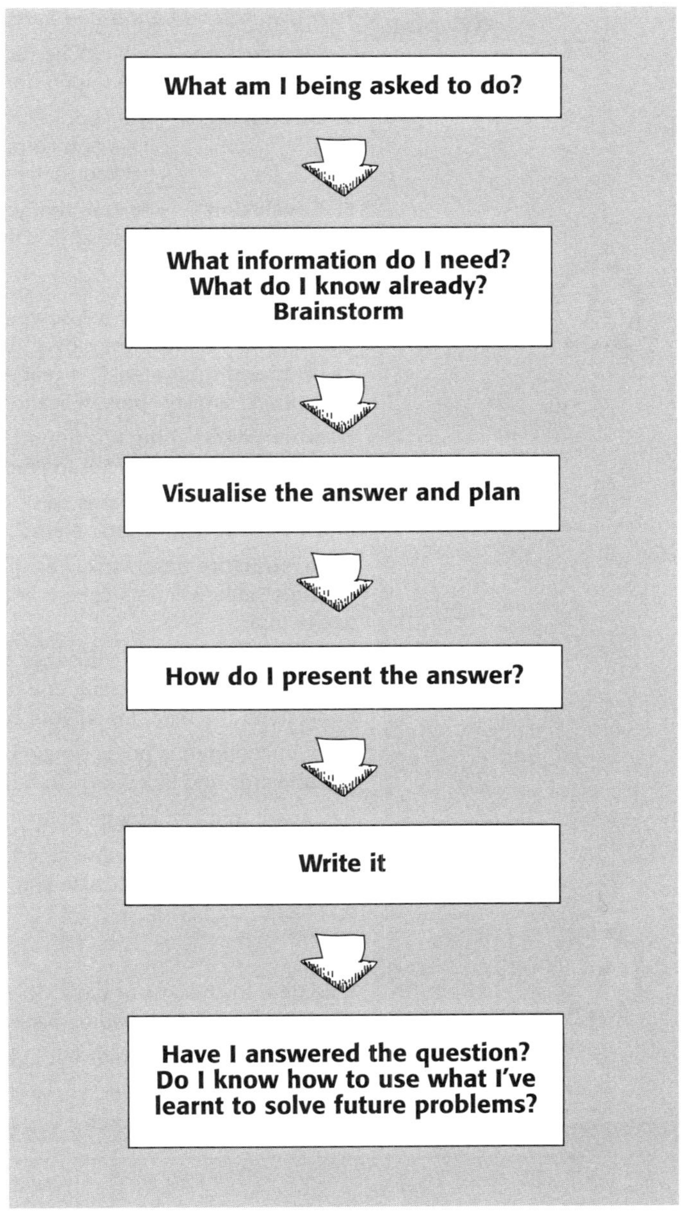

# ★ The basic principles of written assignments

**E — Evaluate the question**

You must consider what the question is asking you to include. (You could also ask yourself what you **shouldn't** put in.) Read the question through two–three times. Can you make the question clearer to you if you rephrase it? Look for key words: 'command' words and 'guide' words (see the list on page 42).

As you work keep looking back at the title to check you are sticking to the point.

**S — Select information and resources**

Consider all the resources available to you (see page 20). Don't rush; careful work now will save you time later.

Make brief notes of your ideas.

Try to create links and comparisons between points.

Put all your points in order.

Only include relevant material.

Ask yourself: 'Is this information useful – is it really needed? How can I use it?'

**S — Sketch and structure the plan**

You must plan your answer. There are various ways of doing this, for example using: flow chart, summary brainframes, linear plans, lists or paragraph headings (see pages 36–37).

Your plan should be in three parts:

1. **Introduction** – you will be required to define the question and set the scene. Remember first impressions are very important.
2. **Development** – you should consider how many paragraphs and in what order. Try to show links and comparisons. You should look for a balanced argument that is backed up by facts, quotations and evidence.
3. **Conclusion** – be sure that you summarise and provide an answer, and you need to tie up loose ends. Only add your opinion if it is required.

**A — Accurately write it**

**Imagery** You should try to use your imagination to help the reader 'visualise' what you mean. It will help you express your ideas better, be more creative and allow the reader to be more involved and motivated. The reader can be involved in a multisensory way. For example, use metaphors, similies, personification, alliteration and onomatopoeia.

**Handwriting/spelling** It is important to make sure that what you write can be read. Handwriting that is difficult to read and key words misspelt will damage your eventual result.

**Illustrations and diagrams** can be a particularly effective way of making a point. You should practise them before your exams. They should support your answer, not replace it.

**Style, structure and clarity** Paragraphs made up of several sentences, normally, following one theme or idea will help convey your 'message'. All the sentences in the paragraph should relate to the topic.

Each paragraph should introduce the next step in your answer. These should be linked in a logical order. Check spelling and punctuation as you go. Punctuation helps the reader understand the meaning of your work.

Write in continuous prose or use bullet points, subheadings and so on if this acceptable. Use signal words and link words to help you (see page 42).

Be careful to avoid repetition and bias.

Think about who you are writing for and try to excite their interest but remember it must be clear and direct. Just because you have to write in a formal manner doesn't mean to say your text has to be boring!

**Y — You must proof read**

Take time to check your work. This is called proof reading and is very important but surprisingly often neglected. (Try reading backwards to notice spelling mistakes.)

Imagine you're the marker – it helps you focus on the sense of your answer.

Look for the mistakes you know you normally make. You need to learn from your mistakes! Carelessness now could cost you exam marks.

# ★ Presentation skills

*The look of your coursework, homework and your exam work will be greatly improved if you also plan how you are going to present it.*

Think again about how the brain likes to receive information. It likes visual images, diagrams, colour, and descriptive sentences using metaphors and similes. It also likes ordered, easy to follow, step-by-step writing, so that the information links together and makes sense. It likes easy to read handwriting and proper paragraphing.

Think about it ... if you were marking a piece of work, wouldn't all of the above be important to you?

*Above all, try to make your work look attractive*

***Here are some points to consider:***

- vary your presentation if you are allowed to
- break up work with illustrations and diagrams or labelled charts
- don't completely replace words with pictures – these should be used to emphasise your written point
- don't write in very long sentences
- use colour in your coursework or revision notes so that your work is eye-catching
- practise making diagrams and think about titles or information you will need to give them

If you are presenting coursework or a project that will make up a part of your exam marks check this list with your teacher:

- should it be bound?
- can you use a word processor?
- should you write on both sides?
- do you need double margins?
- are you allowed to illustrate?
- should you include a contents and index page?

***Ways of varying the presentation without using diagrams or illustrations are:***

- using bullet points or asterisks
- using headings and subheadings
- shading
- changing your font: use *italics*, **bold** or CAPITAL LETTERS
- laying out examples and quotes in a different and attractive way

*Follow a logical pattern and remember to keep it simple – you can actually make the text harder to read if you introduce too much variety.*

## ★ Understanding the question

These are the key words in titles or questions. To answer successfully you need to focus on these and know what they mean. They're called **approach** or **command** words. Highlight them when you are studying the question.

**Key words in titles or questions**

| | |
|---|---|
| **Account for** | explain and examine the main points |
| **Analyse** | examine component parts |
| **Compare** | look for similarities/differences |
| **Contrast** | set in opposition to bring out differences |
| **Criticise** | Make a judgement of facts or opinion, through reasoned discussion and supported with evidence |
| **Define** | set down the precise meaning of word, phrase, topic |
| **Discuss** | investigate/examine through argument for and against; debate |
| **Describe** | give a detailed account |
| **Differentiate/ Distinguish** | look for differences between |
| **Enumerate** | list or specify and describe |
| **Evaluate** | make an appraisal of the worth of something |
| **Explain** | make plain; interpret the meaning of |
| **Interpret** | make clear and explicit |
| **Illustrate** | make clear and explicit |
| **Justify** | show adequate grounds for decision/conclusions |
| **Outline** | give main features/general principles |
| **Prove** | demonstrate truth/falsehood with evidence |
| **Relate** | a) narrate b) show connection between events/facts |
| **Review** | a) survey b) criticise |
| **State** | present in brief, uncomplicated form |
| **Summarise** | make a concise account of the main points omitting detail and example |
| **Trace** | follow the development of the topic |

**Link words**

These words help you to link your ideas in a logical way:

| | |
|---|---|
| **to begin** | firstly; the purpose of this report is ... |
| **to add** | furthermore; moreover; meanwhile; then |
| **to illustrate** | for example; that is; to clarify; for instance |
| **to contrast** | alternatively; however; on the other hand |
| **to finish** | to conclude; finally; therefore; thus; ultimately |

**Signal words**

If you wish your answer to be easy to follow and the points to stand out try some of these:

**vital; outstanding; crucial; significant; fundamental; important**.

Avoid repeating the same words too often – and remember words such as 'basically' often suggest you haven't really thought about how to express yourself.

## ★ Essay Review

**A checklist to follow when you are producing a written assignment.**

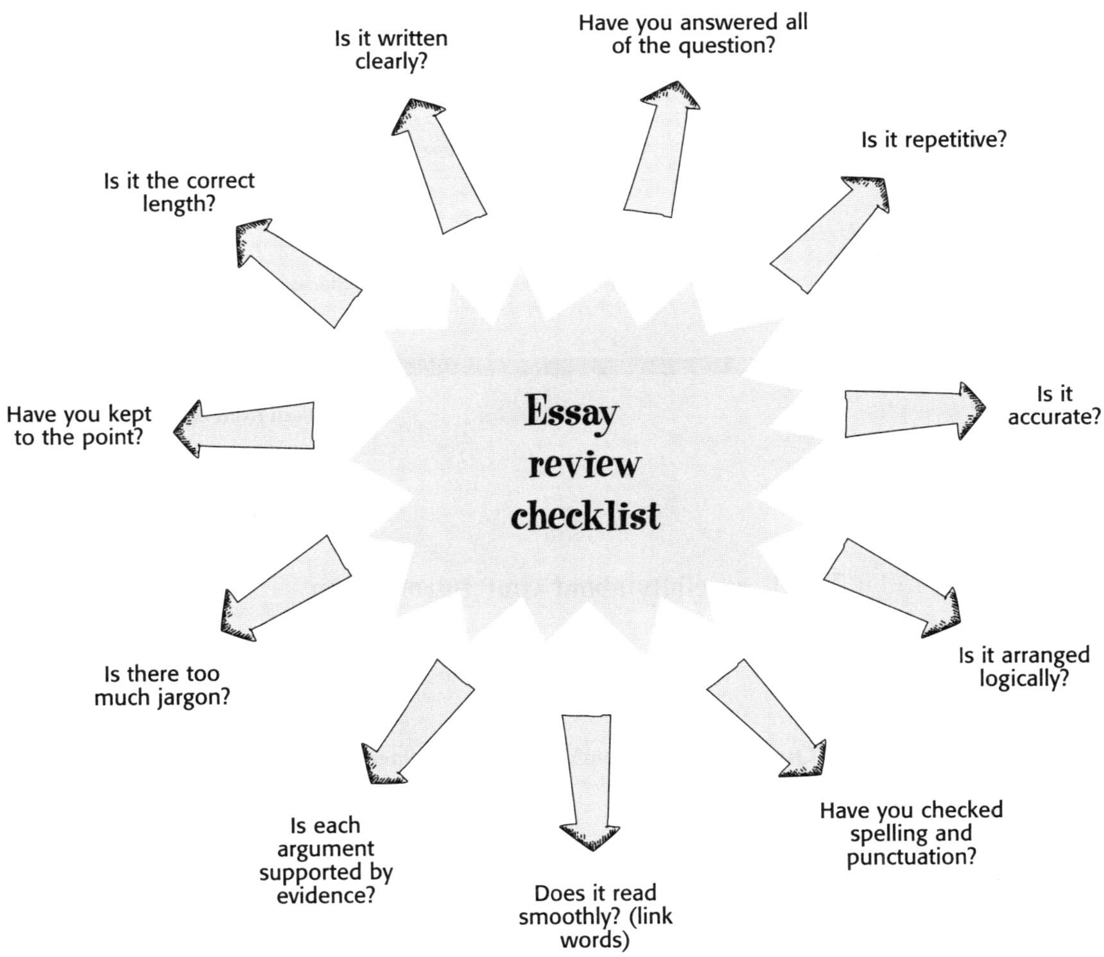

# Good examples

## Plan your essays

**Using a flow chart**

Some people prefer to make a **flow chart**. By doing this they can keep their options open, and let their ideas flow for a longer period before they become set into a fixed form. Figure 11.1 is a flow chart made by a student preparing to write after reading Harper Lee's *To Kill a Mocking Bird*. He wanted to write about prejudice in the story and began by putting his ideas down quickly as they came to him.

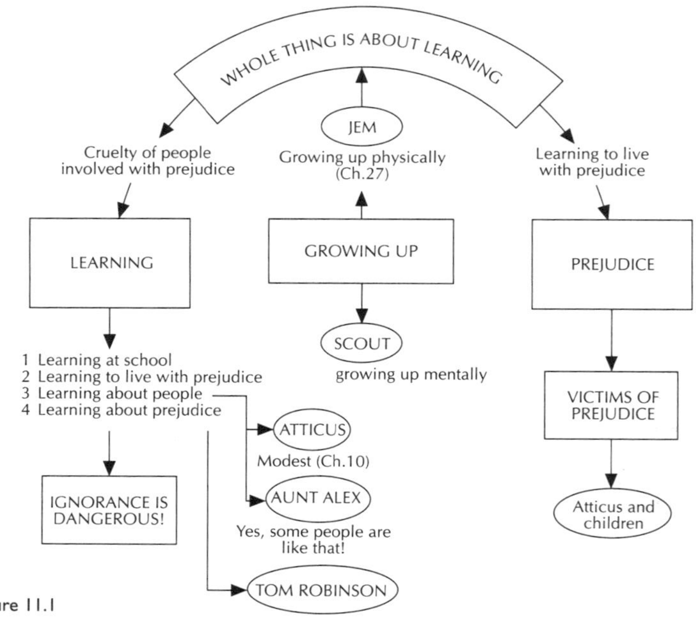


Figure 11.1

If you make a chart, it is a good idea to discuss it with a friend, or make one as a group.

**Taken from *Longman Study Guide: GCSE English*, p. 123**

## Think carefully about your introduction

**Question 3** ***Student's answer – examiner's comment***

'An efficient, if obvious introduction.'

Arms and the Man *is a play illustrating how different characters think, react and respond to numerous aspects on love and war, what they learn from each other throughout the play, and how their opinions and decisions would have, and eventually do, affect their lives.*

*(continued)*

**Taken from *Longman Study Guide: GCSE English Literature*, p. 127**

**Question**

For a motorway lamp, the length of the motorway lit by the lamp is equal to two-thirds of the height of the lamp

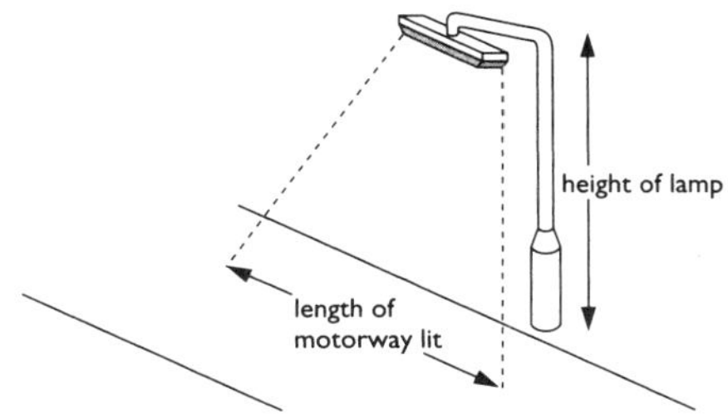


(a) Copy and complete the following table.

'Good, all correct'

| *Lamp* | *Height (metres)* | *Length lit (metres)* |
|---|---|---|
| X | 6 | *4* |
| Y | *9* | 6 |

(b) Two X lamps are positioned 6 metres apart. What length of motorway is unlit between the lamps?

*1 metre*

'Poor answer as it is wrong and there is no indication of how the answer has been found'

(c) Two Y lamps are positioned 5 metres apart. Draw a diagram showing clearly the section of the motorway lit by *both* lamps. How long is this section?

'Again, the answer is incomplete. There are no measurements'

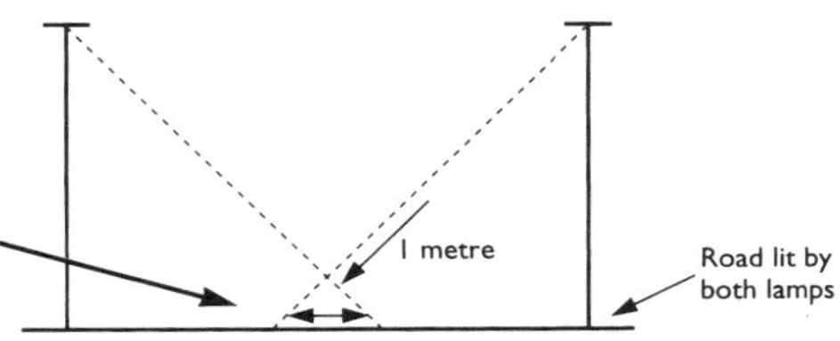


(d) The cost of a lamp, in pounds, is given by:

Cost = 700 + (175 × height) where the height is measured in metres

Find the cost of lamps X and Y.

*X = 700 + (175 × 6) = £1750*

*Y = 700 + (175 × 9) = £2275*

'Good, both parts are correct'

(e) A planning officer is trying to decide what lamps to buy for a new motorway junction of total length 100 metres. She has to make sure that the whole length of the junction will be lit and that the total cost is as low as possible. Should she buy lamps X or lamps Y? Explain your answer fully.

*100 m. Cost of X =* $\frac{100}{4}$ *= 25 × 1,750 = £43,750*

*100 m. Cost of Y =* $\frac{100}{6}$ *= 16.67 × 2,275 = £37,916.51*

*It will be cheaper to buy Y lamps.*

'Good answer, except that the 16.67 should have been rounded up in the calculation'

**Taken from *Longman Study Guide: GCSE Mathematics*, p. 57**

(a) Titanium(IV) chloride is a simple molecular covalent substance. It is a liquid at room temperature. Given that the titanium atom has four outer electrons used for bonding, draw a diagram to show the bonding in titanium(IV) chloride (only the outer electrons of the chlorine atoms should be shown).

'An excellent start—but why did you miss out the electrons around three of the chlorine atoms? You must give a complete set'

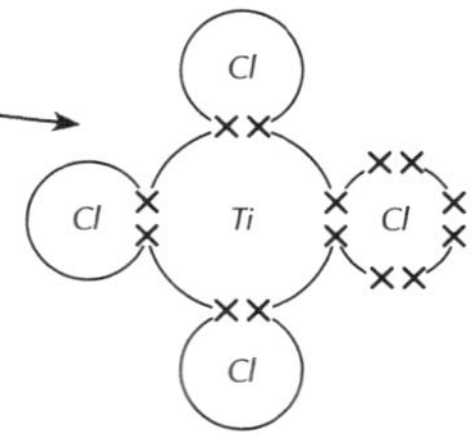


*(2 marks)*

(b) Write a balanced equation for the reaction of titanium(IV) chloride with sodium.

*$TiCl_4$ + 4Na → Ti + 4NaCl*

'Correct'

*(1 mark)*

(c) Suggest a reason why it is necessary to carry out the reaction of titanium(IV) chloride with sodium in an atmosphere of argon.

*Sodium would react with most other gases—argon is inert.*

'Almost right. If air was present sodium would oxidize'

*(1 mark)*

(d) (i) Explain why the physical state of titanium(IV) chloride differs from that of sodium chloride at room temperature.

*titanium chloride is a simple molecular compound but sodium chloride is ionic.*

'Worth a mark out of two. You give, correctly, the structures of the compounds but do not explain why they are liquid or solid. Molecules have weak forces of attraction between them. Sodium chloride is an ionic giant structure with strong forces of attraction leading to the solid state'

(ii) Do you consider that electrolysis of the liquid titanium(IV) chloride would be a suitable method for obtaining titanium?
Give a reason.

*No, because titanium chloride is molecular and would not conduct electricity.*

'Good. Spot on!'

*(3 marks)*
*(continued)*

*(continued)*

(e) Titanium is expensive in spite of the fact that it is relatively abundant in the Earth's crust. Suggest a reason for this.

*It must cost a lot to extract. If sodium or magnesium is needed they would both be expensive.*

'A good answer.'

*(1 mark)*

(f) Use your knowledge of magnesium and the information in the question to explain

(i) how TWO properties of magnesium makes it less suitable than titanium for spacecraft construction

*Its melting point is quite low so it would melt on re-entering the atmosphere.*

'Difficult to find a second property? Spacecraft carry oxygen as a fuel and also for the space crew. In a fire, magnesium + oxygen would be a very dangerous combination!'

(ii) how ONE property of magnesium makes it suitable for aircraft construction

*low density.*

'Yes'

*(4 marks)*
*(Total 12 marks)*

'Overall a good answer which might score 8/12'

**Taken from *Longman Study Guide: GCSE Chemistry*, p. 119–20**

## ▷ Question 2(c) *Student answer with examiner's comments*

'So, how did this help to end McCarthyism?'

'So, was it a mistake to attack public figures, and did his committee's appearance on TV enhance or damage his reputation?'

> *In 1953 the Korean War came to an end. McCarthy attacked important public figures and his committee was shown in action on TV. He decided to accuse a general of communism. Eisenhower, although of the same political party, did not like McCarthy. Many people in the USA were rather ashamed of the way in which they had supported the communist 'witch-hunt'.*

'Was this a mistake?'

'These points require explanation and development.'

*Examiner's decision on the student answer*

A brief answer, in which no reasons appear at the beginning, but reasons are hinted at towards the end. The student knows something, but fails to make use of the knowledge. This would be only Level 2 at about 4/10.

## ▷ Question 2(d) *Student answer with examiner's comments*

> *Communism was still feared by most Americans in the 1960s and 1970s. The Cold War was still at its height, the Russians had the hydrogen bomb, and many believed that the Vietnam War was an attempt by the communists to take over the whole of South-East Asia. Spy-planes, soon to be replaced by spy-satellites, heightened the tension, but World War Three did not seem as close as it had during the Korean War. The humiliation of withdrawal from Vietnam in the early 1970s made the Americans even more rather than less determined to face up to the challenge of communism and to prevent its expansion both internationally and at home.*

*Examiner's decision on the student answer*

This is still rather brief, but is more sharply focused than (c). It needs more development, and would not achieve the highest Level. It would probably be Level 3, scoring about 7/10.

**Taken from *Longman Study Guide: GCSE World History*, p. 203**

# Proof read your answers

Here is an example of a piece of a student's work corrected, using the marks given in Table 20.1.

| Meaning of mark | Mark in text | Mark in margin |
|---|---|---|
| Word or letter left out | ⁁ | ⁁ plus word or letter |
| Full stop left out | ⁁ | ⊙ |
| Comma left out | ⁁ | ⁁ |
| Question mark left out | ⁁ | ? |
| Quotation marks left out | ⁁ | ⁁ |
| Apostrophe left out | ⁁ | ⁁ |
| Change to capitals | ≡ | cap |
| Begin a new paragraph | [ | n.p. |
| Run two paragraphs together | ⌒ | run on |
| Figures or abbreviations to be spelt out | encircle words or figures to be altered | spell out |
| Take out | / | ∂ |

Table 20.1

*Moving House*

It was dreadful weather when we moved house of course but as mum said that was only to be expected. The removal men came early they kept tramping through the house, bringing in mud from the garden. They went to and fro, lugging huge packing cases as if they were nothing at all. One labelled Glass – with care was half thrown into the back of the van. Mum said she felt relieved when the van finally drive off. The men seemed very cheerful because half of their work was over but we felt miserable to leave our old house. As the van turned the corner I took a last look at our big apple tree the one where I use to swing on a tyre when I was little. I felt sadder and sadder all the way to the new house. It was only about (5) miles away, but it was in a totally different area. When we got to the new house, it looked horrible through the rain the garden was terribly overgown and the convolvulus was even creeping in at the window. Why did we have to come here, mum? I asked, but she just stared glumly through the car window. It really was an awful first impression.

(Margin marks: cap/ … /handle/ … o/ … r/ d/ … spell out … cap/)

**Taken from *Longman Study Guide: GCSE English*, pp. 209–10**

## Summary of Part Two

# Practical Revision Skills

Consider how best to revise a subject or topic. Ask yourself:

- What do I know already?
- What do I need to know?

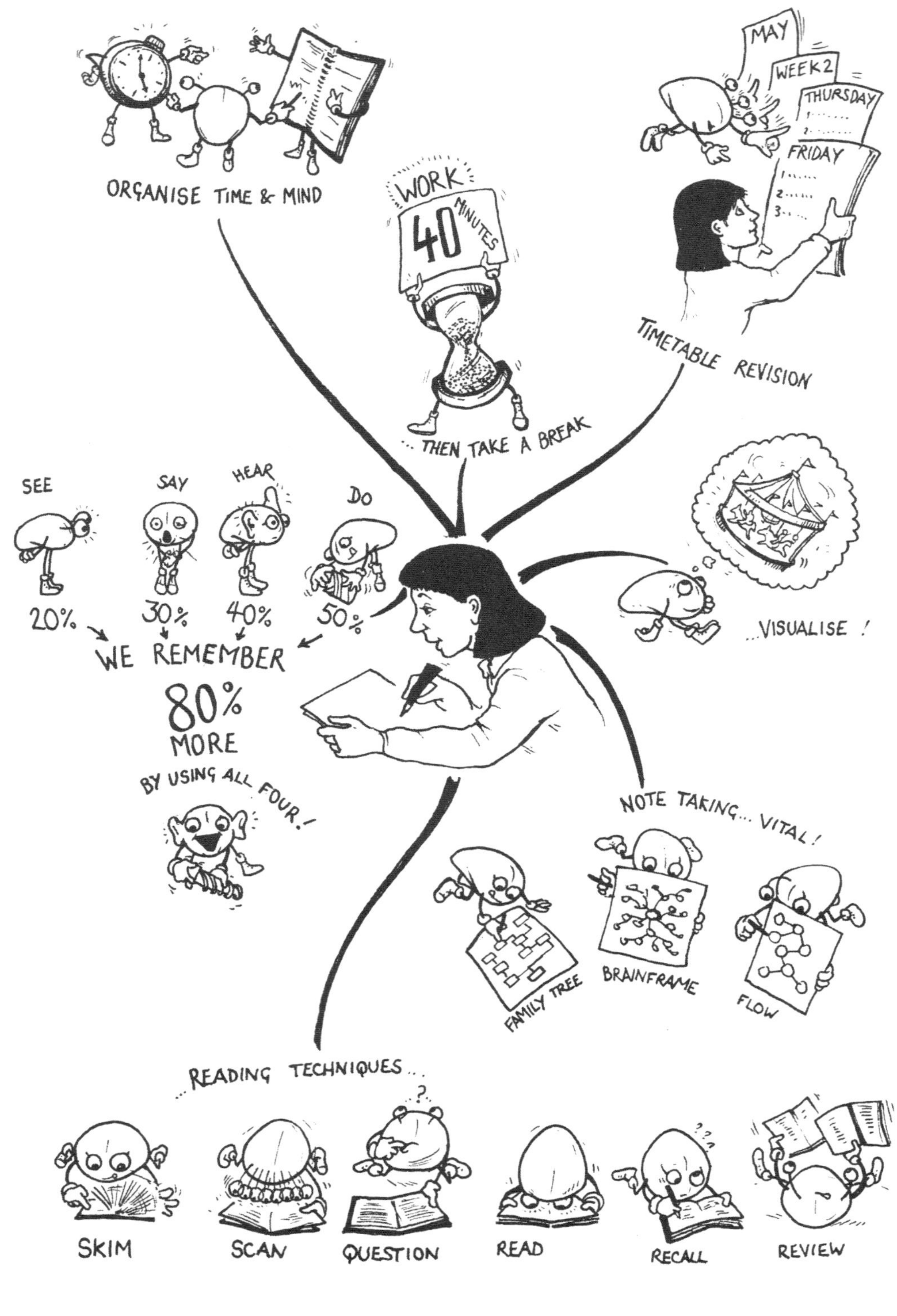

# Part 3
# Practical Exam Skills

*This final section shows you how best to approach the exam in the time leading up to it and on the day of the exam itself. It has many practical tips for coping with exams to maximise your potential.*

# Exam preparation

Exam preparation is a little different from straightforward revision – it's about how you cope with your studies in the days and weeks actually running up to the exam.

When you know the exams are just a few weeks away, focus on your timetable and look through your list of topics. How have you been getting on? What does your teacher consider important for you? How do you think you can further improve? Have you covered each topic in enough depth and have you been reviewing your topics often enough?

## ★ Active revision

*Remember that **active revision** is essential, right up to the exam.*

*Now is a good time to vary your approach when revising.*

**Use your revision action plan:**

1. Revise at a sensible time of day
2. Don't leave out topics
3. Use past papers – learn to recognise questions that are to do with your topics
4. Become familiar with the time each question takes to answer
5. Learn to produce plans on general topics
6. Practise introductions and conclusions
7. Use different methods of revision – essays, class notes, tapes, etc.
8. Use reference or index cards for bite-size chunks of information
9. Work for 30–40 minutes, then break
10. Revise each topic three to four times

## ★ Activating your memory

You need to take advantage of the ways in which you can help your memory retain information:

- intend to remember – your frame of mind as you learn is important
- visualise the information in your mind's eye
- focus on key points/words only – using patterned notes
- add information, colours, illustrations or comments as you go through the text
- identify typical questions – go through the questions you've practised
- sketch answers; try to do this under exam conditions – 'unseen' (this helps you practise drawing on your memory)

### Remember your memory review programme

- skim/scan read; concentrate for a few focused seconds
- talk through **key points** in your head
- learn – intend to learn from notes
- test yourself at the end
- review the topic for 5 minutes in the evening
- review again for 5 minutes in the early morning

## ★ Learn to answer past paper questions

*Always consult your teacher on your practice papers.*

Before you start answering or revising a topic question, ask yourself ...

**What's my purpose?** What's wanted? Is it an essay/report/summary/article/letter/plan? Look at the question command words and guide words.

**What is the expected content?** How long should the answer be? What do I include? What do I leave out? What is the timescale?

**Who is the audience?** What does the examiner expect?

**How is it best produced?** Which style? Which presentation?

## ★ The days leading up to the exam

- Plan your sessions carefully – always ask yourself, 'What do I need to do still?'; 'How can I improve?'; 'How would I answer questions on ...'
- Check all equipment – plan your supplies.
- Allow yourself plenty of relaxation time – practise controlling stress. Plan some 'review' sessions to reassure yourself you're in control.
- Don't revise late into the evening – your final 'intense' review session should not be after 8.00 p.m.
- Find somewhere to exercise, you will need to unwind and work off stress.
- Talk to others and ask for help if you're anxious.
- Find a way to laugh – laughter releases tension.

**In the evenings:**

- overview your topics
- have plenty of relaxation. Try to clear your mind. Be cheerful!
- sleep (you need 8 hours).

## ★ On the day

*Exercise clears your head and refreshes your mind.*

- Wake up early enough to become fully aware and be able to listen and concentrate.
- Stretch to warm up.
- Exercise to freshen up!
- Review all topics for about 5 minutes each.
- Focus on a positive state of mind.
- Have a high energy breakfast and drink water.
- Go for a jog or a swim. Exercise will increase blood flow and oxygen intake and will wake up your brain!

## Equipment

Before you leave home:

check all equipment and supplies

check you have enough pens, pencils, colours, rubber, ruler, and so on

do you need maths equipment, calculator, any texts, dictionary, lucky mascot?

make sure your watch works and is accurate

## Mental preparation

***Your attitude/state of mind***

- Smile!
- Think yourself in the exam ... ask typical questions: 'How would I answer ...?'
- Think of your past successes.
- Remember you know **much more** than you think you do.
- **Relax** and let the knowledge flow.
- Reaffirm venue and time of exams.

*Recognise that you should always remain calm to be at your best.*

***Now do some brain exercises***

- Juggling or doodling with both hands will link both brain hemispheres and increase your concentration before you start the exam.
- The neurovascular points on your forehead, behind your ears and around your temples when rubbed will allow greater focus and concentration.
- You will benefit from a brisk walk and/or some gentle loosening exercises. Stretch, as if warming up for sport and gently roll your neck from side to side – not all the way round, as this can stretch your neck too much.

# The exam

Don't arrive more than 5 minutes before the exam so that you avoid 'panic people'. You'll find it hard to stay calm if you spend much time with these highly-strung folk! Don't arrive exactly **on** time either as you may feel 'late' because others have already entered the exam room.

## ★ Enter the exam room

- Check your desk and chair are comfortable.
- Set out your equipment.
- Relax and focus on the questions and topics you've practised.
- Try some more brain exercises – double doodles.
- Smile (it helps everybody – but don't grin like an idiot).
- Calm down – take a few deep breaths and open your learning channels.
- If in doubt about anything, ask the invigilator.

## ★ Follow instructions

- Listen to the invigilator. (There can be changes to instructions.)
- Fill in Examination Centre details and your name.
- Number the first page.
- Read written instructions carefully, they will tell you: time; choice of questions; type of answer; number of marks.
- Read all the questions. Eliminate those you don't want to do. Choose very carefully because each question deserves time – you may suddenly realise you **can** do it after all.
- Think about a general plan for the exam.

## ★ Timing in the exam

Read the questions two–three times ... slowly. Remember how you've been advised to plan the exam:

*__Draw__ up your plan – perhaps as a pie chart or a list.*

reading time
planning time
time for each answer
checking time

**An example of how to plan your exam time**

Planning helps to keep you calm and in control.

***What happens if you don't plan your time?***

- You rush answers and panic.
- You leave answers or miss obvious questions.
- Your memory doesn't react – so you begin to feel worried.

***What happens if you fall behind in your plan?***

- Don't panic: reduce each answer time – you **can** do it!
- Go into note form if absolutely necessary.
- Try to finish **each** question – show your working out if you have to.

*It is normal for you to have to readjust your plan in the exam from time to time. We all do! If you have practised readjusting your plan beforehand you will find it doesn't completely throw you.*

## Planning and answering the questions

***You should have had plenty of practice at this!***

- The type of plan doesn't matter. You can use: patterned notes, spidergrams, flow diagrams, paragraph headings or linear plans.
- You need to plan how much time you can devote to each answer. Allow time for **checking**.
- Plan in quiet reflection time between questions. A couple of minutes to take stock will help you maintain focus, concentration and allow you to unwind a little.
- Look for **key words** in questions – command and guide words. What does the examiner want?
- Look back at the section on written assignments (page 39). You should concentrate on: **Introduction**, **Development** and **Conclusion**.
- Try to put your points in an ordered, logical way (planning the answer will help with this).
- While sticking to your time plan and action plan you also need to relax and write freely – let it flow.
- If you are allowed to, drink some water every now and again.
- If eating is permitted, boost your energy with a banana or mini Mars.
- Stretches and brain exercises (page 14) can help your flow and release tension.

## What is a 'good answer'?

- Well revised.
- Shows you have understood the question.
- Planned.
- Flows, is clear and makes sense.
- Visually interesting.
- Answers the question asked.
- Shows all the necessary workings.
- Concluded and checked.
- Calculated to gain as many marks as possible.
- Leaves you feeling satisfied you've done a good job!

### *What happens if your mind goes blank and you begin to panic?*

Remember how your brain works. If you **allow** yourself to panic you will close your middle and higher brain and therefore you'll have even less chance of remembering anything. Panic and anxiety will also lessen your chances of choosing the right question.

What to do if you feel panic:

- relaxation techniques do help – stretch; take deep breaths; rub the neurovascular points on your forehead
- don't spend too long trying to remember a point – leave a space or a line. Come back to it later.
- keep writing any ideas or thoughts on rough paper
- ask yourself questions – who, why, where, when, how, what happened, what resulted – then try again

> *Remember – you **do** know it. If it is a very difficult question relax and resolve to give your best. Once you are calmer it is amazing how you will suddenly remember the information you need.*

### *In between exams if you have two on one day*

- Get some fresh air – and move around.
- Have lunch for about 20 minutes then freshen up.
- Then spend 30 minutes on a **focused review** (think about typical questions).
- Relax. Try some more brain exercises and positive thinking.
- Close your eyes and treat the afternoon as a 'new day'.

## ★ Post mortems

### *Is a 'post mortem' a good idea?*

Should you go through an exam immediately afterwards to assess your success rate? On balance, no. You do gain plenty of reassurance if you've done well. But if you discover you've done badly you will be highly demotivated and it will possibly affect how you do in other exams.

Look to the future and don't spend time getting worked up about the past. What's done is done.

> *You've tried your best – and because you've followed the advice in this book you haven't relied on luck alone. In fact, you have made your own luck!*

## Summary of Part Three

# Practical Exam Skills

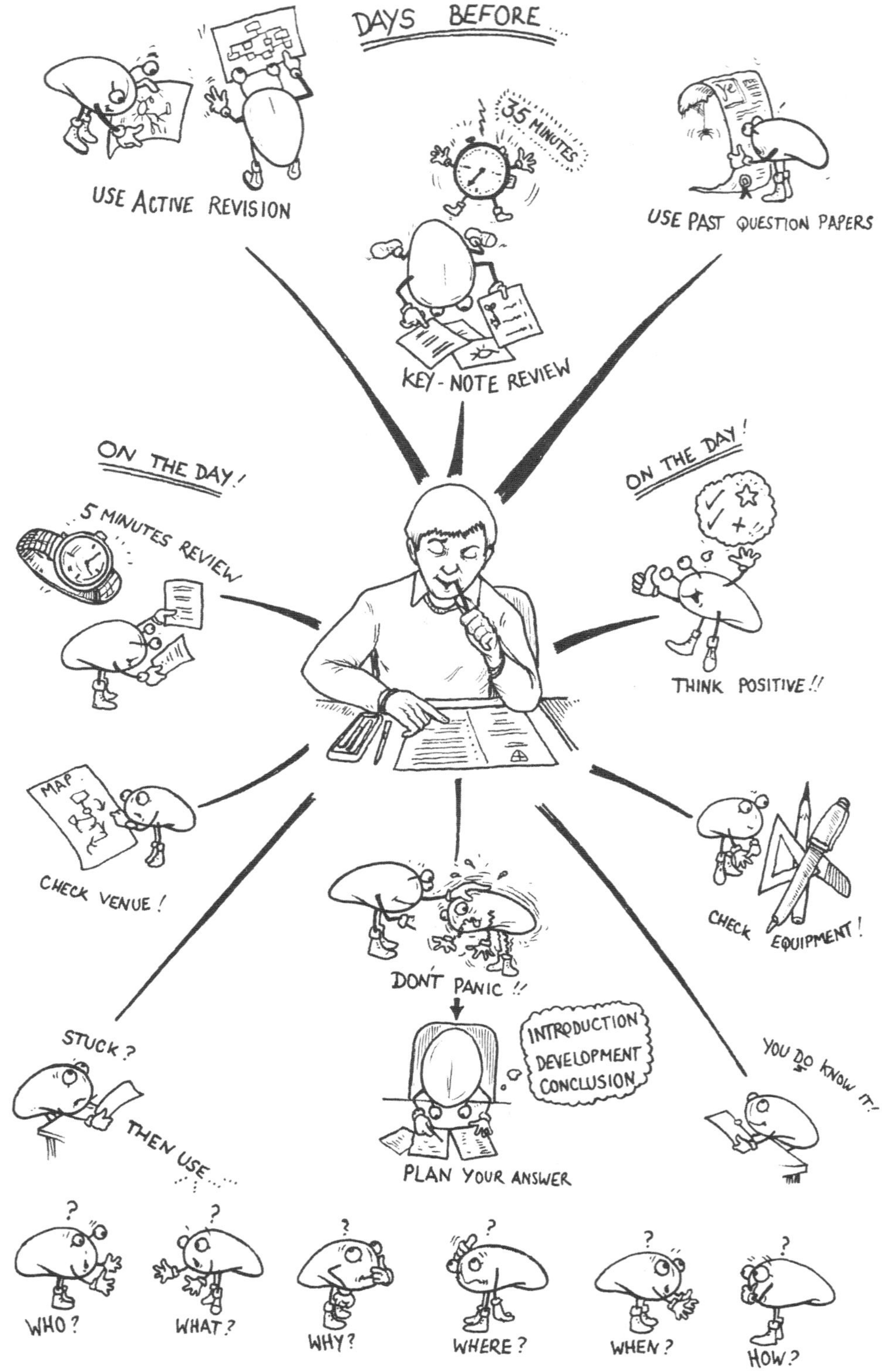

# Action plan

Go back to each section and pick ideas, suggestions and techniques that appeal to you. Then create at least **three objectives** that you intend to achieve from that section. So, for example, for *Maximise your brain power* on pages 2–5, one of your objectives might be:

- *I intend to learn using multisensory skills, including my visual, auditory and practical ones.*

## Part One Brain Power

**Maximise your brain power**

1. ..........
2. ..........
3. ..........

**Multisensory revision**

1. ..........
2. ..........
3. ..........

**Mind power**

1. ..........
2. ..........
3. ..........

**Mind and body harmony**

1. ..........
2. ..........
3. ..........

## Part Two Practical Revision Skills

**Your learning environment**

1. ..........
2. ..........
3. ..........

**Organising time and mind**

1. ..........
2. ..........
3. ..........

**Revision sessions**

1. ..........
2. ..........
3. ..........

***Memory skills***

1. ..................................................................
2. ..................................................................
3. ..................................................................

***Reading and learning***

1. ..................................................................
2. ..................................................................
3. ..................................................................

***Listening skills***

1. ..................................................................
2. ..................................................................
3. ..................................................................

***Note taking***

1. ..................................................................
2. ..................................................................
3. ..................................................................

***Written answers***

1. ..................................................................
2. ..................................................................
3. ..................................................................

***Good examples***

1. ..................................................................
2. ..................................................................
3. ..................................................................

## Part Three Practical Exam Skills

***Exam preparation***

1. ..................................................................
2. ..................................................................
3. ..................................................................

***The exam***

1. ..................................................
2. ..................................................
3. ..................................................